Who Touched Base in My Thought Shower?

A Treasury of Unbearable Office Jargon

STEVEN POOLE

SCEPTRE

First published in Great Britain in 2013 by Sceptre
An imprint of Hodder & Stoughton
An Hachette UK company

1

Copyright © Steven Poole 2013

The right of Steven Poole to be identified as the Author
of the Work has been asserted by him in accordance with the
Copyright, Designs and Patents Act 1988.

A CIP catalogue record for this title is available from the British Library

Hardback ISBN 978 1 444 78184 7
eBook ISBN 978 1 444 78436 7

Typeset in ITC New Baskerville by Hewer Text UK Ltd, Edinburgh
Printed and bound by Clays Ltd, St Ives plc

Hodder & Stoughton policy is to use papers that are natural,
renewable and recyclable products and made from wood grown
in sustainable forests. The logging and manufacturing processes
are expected to conform to the environmental regulations
of the country of origin.

Hodder & Stoughton Ltd
338 Euston Road
London NW1 3BH

www.sceptrebooks.co.uk

'By means of the spectacle the ruling order discourses endlessly upon itself in an uninterrupted monologue of self-praise' – *Guy Debord*

'I would prefer not to' – *Bartleby the Scrivener*

CONTENTS

PREFACE

Among the most spirit-sapping indignities of modern life is
the relentless battering of workers' ears by the strangled
vocabulary of office jargon. It might even seem to some
innocent souls as though all you need to do to acquire a
high-level job is to learn its stultifying vocabulary, GOING
FORWARD. Office-speak is a maddeningly viral kind of
Unspeak engineered to deflect blame, complicate simple
ideas, obscure problems, and perpetuate power relations.
Fluency in the idiom is a kind of cheap competence (or
COMPETENCY) that often masks a lack of competence in
anything that matters.

Now, there's nothing wrong with jargon per se. You
can't discuss quantum physics, for example, or the technical aspects of musical composition, without specialized
terms that are incomprehensible to outsiders. The paradoxical thing about modern office jargon, though, is that it
is a specialized language that is supposedly applicable to
absolutely everything – whether the office in question is in
the field of broadcasting, advertising, manufacturing,
banking, charitable fundraising, or anything else. Having
noticed this, one might become rather suspicious about its
alleged necessity. (Just as some insiders – such as former
consultant Matthew Stewart in *The Management Myth* – are
sceptical about the worth of 'management theory' itself.)

When I first wrote about this abusive argot in 2013, my article became the most viewed page on the *Guardian* network globally, and within hours there were thousands of comments from frustrated office workers offering examples of their own pet verbal hates. Intriguingly, they spoke of their reaction to such language in terms of violence and illness. When they hear such buzzwords in the workplace, they want to stab someone in the eye with a pen, or they feel physically sick.

Workers resent in particular the emotional blackmail of modern office-speak, particularly the horrid cluster of TEAM-talk. Modern work, indeed, involves not just actual labour (being told to ACTION the DELIVERABLES), but emotional labour as well. Employees of the fast-food chain Prêt à Manger are required to perform a list of 'Prêt Behaviours' that include 'has a sense of fun' and 'is happy to be themself' (*sic*). Prêt workers are even encouraged to touch one another a lot. The workplace thus now insists on what Slavoj Žižek calls 'the superego injunction to enjoy' – not only must you do your job, you must actually be happy to do it, or at least be able to present a seamless simulacrum of doing so.

While people are increasingly ordered to be happy and think of their work as a kind of playtime, the language in which such orders are couched is dispiriting and alienat-ing, prompting fantasies of ocular penetration with writing implements. People feel as though such jargon treats them as objects, just as the ubiquity of the term human resources (and even worse, HUMAN CAPITAL) implies. (As Peppcr

Potts's head of security in *Iron Man Three* enthuses: 'The "human" part of "human resources" is our biggest vulnerability. We need to start phasing it out immediately.') Indeed, it turns out that ordinary people are more linguistically sensitive and discriminating than is often suspected by those who wield the power to choose the official dialect. Inspired by Dilbert, they play 'bullshit bingo' in meetings; they sigh wearily when having to edit reports crammed with such deadening cant; they catch themselves using it too, and quietly despair.

The irresistible rise of modern office jargon has its origin in the beginnings of business theory in the 1950s and 1960s; it was fuelled by the later rise of the discipline of 'project management', and went viral during the dotcom boom of the late 1990s. Now it is everywhere, from cubicle farms that represent real-life versions of TV series *The Office*, to government press releases. (Margaret Thatcher was the rare politician of modern times who did not embrace management jargon: she referred to it with characteristic asperity as 'all this guffy stuff'.) For the past three years, the website of *Forbes* magazine (not commonly thought to be a sneering leftie anti-business operation) has run a 'Jargon Madness' tournament, inviting people to vote on the buzzwords that annoy them most. And yet the front-runners (e.g. in 2012, LEVERAGE) do not magically disappear from business vocabulary.

Perhaps everyone is scared that if they don't speak the same way, no one will take them seriously. Surveys over the last decade have repeatedly found that workers and managers alike claim to hate jargon: one concluded that it 'results in mistrust and encourages a feeling of inadequacy'. But no one is ready to give it up. A 2012 poll found that more than three-quarters of Britons are annoyed by office jargon, but 44 per cent still admit to using it: presumably some of the others were too ashamed to confess. The pollsters speculated that the incontinent buzzphrasing of desperate contestants on *The Apprentice* and *Dragons' Den* had made it even more ubiquitous.

Thrusting executives also need to talk the talk. Patrick Gray, a consultant, told *Forbes*: 'There's a thieves' code in the corporate world: "I'll use words that sound important but make no actual sense and give you the same privilege if you don't call me out on it."' John Rentoul, the witty anti-cant crusader and author of *The Banned List*, suggests that terms such as SYNERGY and THINKING OUTSIDE THE BOX are just 'fancy ways of saying simple things, or saying nothing much at all . . . they are used in the vain hope that their fanciness will convey a dynamism or sophistication that the writer or speaker fears is lacking.' If so, the consequences of this unspoken conspiracy of fear are woeful indeed.

Certainly a lot of office jargon is engineered to jolly its targets along by making the fluorescent-lit days sound more exciting and important. To do so, it steals terms from the military (ON MY RADAR, PUSH THE ENVELOPE, STRATEGY), sport (DEEP DIVE, CLOSE OF PLAY), information technology (DELIVERABLES, DRILL DOWN), or science (OPTICS, PARADIGM SHIFT), while happily abandoning the specific technical meanings that made such words useful in the first place. But office jargon has darker and more brutalizing tendencies, too. This language tends to dehumanize workers, treating them as computers or robots (DOWNLOAD, BANDWIDTH, INTERFACE), at the same time as it forces on them a kind of wheedling, unwelcome intimacy (TOUCH BASE, REACH OUT), condescends to them as if they were children (BUCKETS, HANDS AND FEET), and obscures management responsibility for things that have gone wrong or might go wrong in the future (GOING FORWARD, ISSUES, RISK). It is at its most insistently creative, tellingly, when dreaming up euphemisms for sacking people (DEMISING, RESIZING), which makes office jargon a kind of wonderfully impermeable condom for the executive conscience.

What is the TAKEAWAY from all this; what are the LEARNINGS? The jargon is all around, yet there is a groundswell of popular loathing for it. We need to be PROACTIVE and fire up a linguistic resistance movement. DRILLING DOWN with the power tools of etymological understanding and merciless ridicule, we can all fight back against the filthy tide of verbal slurry that treats us like idiotic automata every day. Scorn is our best weapon. Workers of the world, unite: you have nothing to lose but your CREATIVE ABRASION.

across the piece

In 2013, the shadow chancellor, Ed Balls, implied that an
incoming Labour government would look at cutting
pensions. 'The majority of most welfare spending is in fact
going to people over sixty,' he said. 'That's the truth and
we should look *across the piece.*'

Across the *what*? *What* the piece? The piece of *what*?
The peculiarly common *across the piece* means simply
'throughout' or 'everywhere', but it seems that no one
knows quite why. *Across the piste* is often heard, as though
people or fencers made a foolish habit of skiing or
fighting sideways, but this is a minority variant of much
more recent origin: it's probably a simple mishearing, or
an attempt (ironically mistaken) to sound more sophisticated. (*Piste* is French, innit?)

Synonymous with the business use of *across the piece* is the
phrase 'across the board', whose origin is said to lie in what
the British call an 'each-way bet' in horse-racing (the
'board' is the bookmaker's). Why 'board' might have given
way to 'piece' in modern office-talk is mysterious, unless it
was thought offensive to wooden people such as the Ents,
Tolkien's talking trees.

What seems to me the likeliest origin is the sense of
'piece', venerable in English, that means an area of
enclosed or otherwise demarcated land (as in the park in

Cambridge called Parker's Piece). The phrase *across the piece* is used in just this sense in William Gilpin's *Observations on the River Wye* of 1782, where he points out glumly that nature rarely offers a completely harmonious composition to the eye: 'Either the foreground or the background is disproportioned; or some awkward line runs across the piece; or a tree is ill-placed; or a bank is formal; or something or other is not exactly what it should be.'

Slightly later, *across the piece* was also used in the context of practical matters, such as in an 1807 printing patent (which offers variation of the pattern 'by changing the order of figures *across the piece*') or in Edward H. Knight's 1874 *The Practical Dictionary of Mechanics*, which defines a 'traverse-saw' as 'a cross-cutting saw which moves on ways *across the piece*'. Perhaps from there *across the piece* came to mean 'covering the whole width' – of anything at all, rather than just a piece of lumber.

This is one example of office-talk that has gone viral in the world of politics too. As though participating in some sort of secret jargon-deployment competition, the virtuosic under-secretary at the Ministry of Justice, Jonathan Djanogly MP, managed in a single answer to the Public Administration Select Committee's 2012 hearings on justice administration to use *across the piece* an impressive four times. He understood why people wanted 'to have some kind of policy format *across the piece*'; he reported that 'we can look *across the piece* in terms of where these tribunals actually sit' and that 'we now have the ability to look *across the piece* in terms of judicial careers'; and he reassured the committee members that 'we are now looking at courts and tribunals *across the piece.*' Impressive!

In discussing welfare spending, Ed Balls could easily have said, 'We should look at all options' or 'We should consider everything.' Unfortunately he spurted, as though it came quite naturally to him: 'We should look *across the piece*' – and so alienated countless voters who are constitutionally allergic to the cliquey argot of managerialese.

action

Some people loathe verbings (where a noun begins to be used as a verb) on principle, though 'text me' is a lot easier to say than 'send me a text'. What about the queasy office verbing *to action*? In his *Dictionary of Weasel Words*, the Australian doyen of management-jargon mockery Don Watson defines *to action* simply as 'do'. This is not quite right: someone asking you to *action* an email is not asking you to 'do' it but to reply to it, or do what it asks, et cetera. The office *action* can probably always be replaced with a more specific verb, such as 'reply' or 'fulfil', even if they sound less excitingly action-y. Somewhat more useful is the phrase *action item*, by means of which you can refer to anything that needs doing, regardless of the type of action necessary.

It is difficult wholly to despise the business-jargon use of *action*, anyway, since it is used by none other than the espionage novelist extraordinaire Len Deighton in *The Ipcress File*. At least there, its vigorous semantics might be thought appropriate to the cloak-and-dagger doings of a spymaster.

Such is the hunger to develop new and disgusting things to say in the office that we now also have the syllable-stacking construction *actionables*. This means nothing more than 'things to be done', which is also a good translation of the familiar term *agenda*. Mind you, *agenda* comes from

Latin, so some people would despise it simply on that basis. (Including George Orwell, whose lunatic strictures in 'Politics and the English Language' include avoiding all words of classical derivation.)

Personally, I find that trying to say *actionables* makes me feel like my mouth is stuffed with pebbles. If only using office jargon were *actionable* in the sense of leading to a devastating lawsuit.

~

adjacency

Let's innovate through *connected adjacencies*! Let's find some *innovation adjacencies* and create some *adjacent innovation platforms* in order to make some *adjacency moves* to usher in a new era of *radical adjacency*. You with me?

We all know, of course, that 'adjacent' means 'next to'. Presumably the office-jargon of *adjacencies* means something more technical and interesting than merely 'things that are next to another thing'? Actually, that's just what it means. An *adjacency* is a market that is somehow 'close' to yours, which you could move into. If you make lawn-mowers, why not move into the garden furniture business too? Simples!

More exciting is the concept of a *radical adjacency*, whose inspirational rhetoric (notice how business language appropriates the left-wing vocabulary of radicalism, revolution and so on) masks an odd contradiction. A *radical adjacency* is an adjacency that, er, is not really that adjacent. As an educational *Forbes* article explains, the company Jawbone is 'evolving a *radical adjacency* strategy'. How so? 'Jawbone makes mobile speakers. It has moved into the medical device and monitoring market.' Radical, man. But not really, you know, all that *adjacent*?

~

air cover

'We need *air cover* on this' is not literally a call for a couple of F16s to roar overhead and unloose a payload of missiles, but just a way of saying that something needs signing off by senior management. Not only is this military metaphor flattering to the people who say it, who are thereby portrayed as kick-ass grunts on the ground, but also – and perhaps more importantly – it's a nice little piece of rhetorical ass-kissing. Senior management, after all, are probably quite pleased to be portrayed as elite fighter pilots, spending the whole day snapping towels at each other, *Top Gun*-style, in a steamed-up locker room.

~

aligning

Aligning is getting two things lined up, or one thing pointing in the right direction towards another. Seems normal enough. *Alignment* happens to turntables and antennae and no one complains. But the use of the term in business seems to upset people, including a number of American executives polled in 2008 who offered it as one of their most annoying buzzwords.

One reason might be that it sounds so neutral – a mere operation of geometry – and so can be deployed as a mealy-mouthed reason for why bad things (e.g. TRANSITIONING) need to happen down the road. As one *Guardian* commenter puts it: 'When an American with an MBA starts talking about *aligning* this with that, you know there's going to be blood on the carpet.'

An equally good reason to resist *alignment*, meanwhile, is that the things being *aligned* are often purely abstract notions that don't naturally have any sides or direction they point in, and so can't strictly be *aligned* at all. When people start babbling about the need to *align* 'goals' or 'values' or 'philosophies', then the concept of *alignment* is just, as *Forbes* puts it, a 'gratingly pretentious version of agreement'. It's more vacuous still when it is actually impossible to tell what, if anything, is being *aligned*, as in a 2013 Microsoft memo that promised the company would be 'Organizing for Speed and Strategic *Alignment*'. (Of *what*, pray tell?)

I am told that a fine way to end a meeting is for everyone to agree: 'We are *aligned*.' But utter disaster is indicated if anyone pipes up to point out: 'Hang on, we're *not aligned*!' One does hope that, at least once, an infuriated employee somewhere has offered to *align* his fist with his boss's face.

~

annual leave

When even the word *holiday* is thought to sound too frivolous and hedonistic, so that people on their holidays set their out-of-office autoreply to announce grandly that they are instead on *annual leave*, then surely we have entered a hellishly self-parodic downward spiral of capitalist civilization?

~

around

'Let's talk *around* X' is a peculiarly passive-aggressive way to suggest a conversation, implying that to talk directly *about* X would be too confrontational. It holds out the promise of an interminable meeting in which everything *around* the subject is discussed at length, while the subject itself is left serenely untroubled by any useful interrogation. The Australian lawyer and writer Michael Teys has noticed corporate constructions such as 'Our seminar tomorrow is *around* the aftermath of the global financial crisis', and an increasing use of *around* in political language as well: in 2010 'the newly elected Greens member for Melbourne called for a debate "*around*" legalising same-sex marriages.' Why not have a debate *about* it? Teys also offers the example, 'We have been doing some work *around* your finances', which I suspect should probably be construed as: 'We haven't actually been working *on* your finances but we're going to bill you anyway.'

Revealingly, to 'talk *around* the subject' in ordinary language means to be evasive, to avoid the point. Perhaps secretly that is what everyone really wants to do: to give the appearance of discussing something without actually having to tackle the real ISSUE. (Of course, where there are ISSUES, they are never issues *about* something but only issues *around* something too.) The cowardly office use of *around*, then, is a fine example of circumlocution squared.

~

ask, the

What is *the ask* here? It's the thing asked-for, the request. (It has been possible to use *ask* as a noun in this way since AD 1000 or so.) Our modern usage seems to have crossed into business parlance from its more specific context in fundraising. There, according to an illuminating analysis by Giovanni Rodriguez, the dance of money-chasing is couched in revealingly romantic terms. First, there is the Courtship between fundraiser and rich person, which the fundraiser hopes will result in the Gift. In between these two comes the crucial moment when the fundraiser explicitly asks for a massive pile of cash – and that is the Ask, a moment fraught with as much nuance and potential for embarrassment as its sexual analogue. In the more general office usage, by contrast, *the ask* (e.g. just 'what the client wants') is not so coyly delayed and surrounded by thrilling frisson.

Naturally, *asks* can be asking for more or less. A *big ask*, specifically, seems to have originated in Australian sporting commentary during the 1980s. And you can make requesting a favour from a co-worker sound more winsome and appealing by couching it as *a tiny ask*. Given the potential for unfortunate mishearings, it's probably wise not to criticize another colleague's expansive demands by saying they have a *fat ask*.

~

backfill

After someone has been sacked – sorry, TRANSITIONED – they
tend to leave a person-shaped hole in the landscape of KEY
ACTIONABLES. What do you do with a hole, especially a
person-shaped one that reminds you a bit of a hastily dug
grave? You fill it in – in other words, you *backfill* (verb), or
address the *backfill* (noun).

Originally, *backfill* is an engineering term, meaning to fill
a hole or trench with excavated earth, gravel, sand, or
other material. Now it works to mean 'replacement' or
'replace', e.g. 'We are recruiting for Tom's *backfill*' or 'We
will have to *backfill* Richard.' (That sounds potentially
rather uncomfortable for Richard.) Meanwhile, a job
vacancy that exists to replace an ex-employee, as opposed
to a newly created role, is called a *backfill position*, even if
that sounds more like something an adventurous type
might adopt at an S&M club.

~

bandwidth

'What's your *bandwidth*?' 'Do you have the *bandwidth* for this?' 'Sorry, I don't have the *bandwidth*.' This is how some human beings actually talk, even when they're not dressed up as Marvin the Paranoid Android.

The spatial metaphor of *bandwidth* in computer technology is pretty simple: it's a measurement of how 'wide' the band or data 'pipe' is, and so of how much information can be pumped down it in a given period of time. Hence 'broadband': an internet connection whose bandwidth is broad.

To describe a human being's ability to do more work as his or her *bandwidth*, then, would strictly imply that they are going to have to do more things simultaneously, rather than get something new to do if they finish what they are currently doing early. It might be thought unfortunate, in that case, that the current consensus in psychology and cognitive science is that 'multitasking' – i.e. trying to do several things at once, or maximizing one's *bandwidth* – is counter-productive and leads to worse results.

Calling our ability to work *bandwidth* also seems to imply a weird kind of cyborg envy. No doubt some managers would prefer their inferiors to have no more independence of mind than all the snaking info-tubes that make up the internet. Personally, I don't have *bandwidth*; I have attention and time, and inclination to work. (Well, more often disinclination.)

Business analyst Emma Sheldrick reports: 'We used to get asked to assess our own *bandwidth* so managers could decide who to task with new work.' The right answer to that, for those old enough to remember the hilariously slow modems of decades ago, is, 'Sorry, my *bandwidth* is only 14.4k baud.'

~

benchmarking

If you just mean 'measuring', for pity's sake stop saying *benchmarking*. It was high up on a list of jargon words that the UK's Local Government Association pleaded with councils to stop using in 2009. They didn't pay any attention, naturally. Even the Italians use it now. The temptation is obvious: *benchmarking* sounds as though you are a good-looking scientist conducting rigorous experiments on your business in a hi-tech laboratory, while any idiot can just measure something.

But, you might wonder, what is a *benchmark* anyway? The term came from surveying in the nineteenth century. A surveyor leaves marks around the landscape (notches in trees, walls, etc.) into which an angled piece of metal can be placed to support the levelling staff from which altitude readings are made. The angled metal piece provides a bracket or *bench* for the staff. So a *benchmark* is a fixed reference point.

You might doubt that this helps justify the modern indiscriminate use of the metaphor, with companies that promise they '*benchmark* our coffees', and marketers offering to '*benchmark* success', which sounds like trying to nail jelly to a wall. Meanwhile – in another example of office-speak growing redundant parts, as an ageing potato sprouts doomed shoots – there is now *best practice benchmarking.* This means *benchmarking* to find the BEST PRACTICE. But finding the BEST PRACTICE was always the whole point of business *benchmarking* anyway. So *best practice benchmarking* could without risk be shortened simply to, er, *benchmarking.*

~

best of breed

What is this, a bloody dog show? Or a horse parade? Or a chicken market? (A 1906 advert in that renowned publication *Poultry Topics and Western Poultry News* promises 'cut prices on the *best of breed*'.) The office use of *best of breed* certainly seems to raise hackles.

You'd think that *best of breed* is so obvious a way of saying 'best company or product in a particular category' that annoying office types would have been saying it for as long as writers for kennel magazines have. But the first example I can find is in a technical paper on mechanical engineering from 1974, which explains: 'The selection of a single best concept can be reached by comparison of candidates on a "winner take all" basis, or by comparative selection from a predetermined group of subclasses ("*best of breed*, best in show").' *Best of breed* then seems to have gained popularity in IT ('*best-of-breed* software') and before too long it had spread everywhere, shedding hair on the global carpet. (Often you'll even find, in a company's own hype, that it is providing *best-of-breed* SOLUTIONS.)

It's notably conceited, too: instead of claiming that your product is merely excellent, by calling it *best of breed* you are saying that it really is superior to everything else. Paradoxically, however, there is usually more than one company in a product category claiming to be *best of breed*, and so no one is any the wiser after all, though they might now be at a slightly elevated risk of contracting rabies.

~

best practice

There's something about the phrase *best practice* – to mean the (notionally) optimal way of doing things – that sticks in many people's throats. Is it a subliminally conceited allusion to the use of *practice* to mean the important work of a doctor or an artist? Or is it perhaps the way that calling it *best practice* to begin with brooks no argument about whether this way of doing things is, in fact, *best* after all? It's rather impolite to claim that what someone else has just called *best practice* is stupid. And so the phrase *best practice* shuts down dissent before it can get started.

Best practice is surprisingly new, first recorded by the *OED* in an accounting textbook of 1984. But perhaps the definitive account of what it really means is offered by the business theorist John Kay in his celebrated 1993 work, *Foundations of Corporate Success*. There he explains: 'There is a mechanism for formulating STRATEGY which is apparently simpler than selecting from a menu of generic strategies in the light of a well-formulated assessment of the business environment. That is to look at what other firms do, and copy it. This strategy is more felicitously expressed as adopting *best practice*.'

And so *to adopt best practice* is really a euphemism for a kind of forelock-tugging plagiarism. We're going to slavishly emulate this other company, but we're sure they won't mind, because in doing so we're calling them *best*. Isn't imitation the sincerest form of flattery?

~

Big Hairy Audacious Goal

This is a totally hilarious term for an ambitious business plan, perhaps one so ambitious that it amounts to BOILING THE OCEAN. It bounced on to the linguistic scene in 1994, in a book entitled *Built to Last* by Jim Collins and Jerry Porras. Collins later told *Inc.* magazine that he and his co-author were wondering what to call ambitious long-term goals. Porras suggested the somnolent 'corporate vision', but Collins wanted something that conveyed 'excitement, energy, and envelope-pushing boldness'. What conveys those things best? Why, *Big Hairy Audacious Goal*, of course!

You might wonder, even so, why the big audacious goal also had to be *hairy*. Does the mere fact of being hirsute help to convey excitement, energy, and PUSHING THE ENVELOPE into the hairy goal, like a confused postman at a gorillas' football match? Perhaps the reason is simpler. *Big Hairy Audacious Goal* has since become so gruesomely popular in public 'MISSION statements' by companies and leaders who want to sound like assholes that it is often referred to simply by its initials: BHAG. (Pronounced *bee-hag*, like a witch who commands a swarm of terrible stinging insects.) Without the *hairy* this would be Big Audacious Goal or BAG, and then executives would just sound like they were rhapsodizing about totes and satchels.

Even those who find the sniggering pseudo-comedy of

the phrase depressing can hardly deny that literally hours of fun can be had with it. 'Did you ACTION my *Big Hairy Audacious Goal*?'; 'My *Big Hairy Audacious Goal* is on the BLEEDING EDGE!'; 'I want to take a DEEP DIVE into your *Big Hairy Audacious Goal*!' – and so on, to the endless merriment of all.

~

bio-break

Not all euphemisms are necessarily bad. The creative little phrase *bio-break*, which dates from the 1990s, accomplishes two things: a) it gets round the problem of whether to say 'loo' or 'bathroom' or 'restroom' break, and b) it makes people sound kind of hip and modern, like biotech engineers. Although cynics might say the use of *bio-break* implies that it's only for a couple of minutes every few hours that you are allowed to be a biological life form instead of a jargon-spouting robot.

~

blamestorming

The 1990s tech boom had its own wave of jargon that subsequently passed into regular office-speak, of which *blamestorming* is one example. First recorded around 1997, it means sitting around to discuss why a deadline was missed or a project was a complete shambles, and to pick an individual or department upon whom all the responsibility will be heaped.

No one actually thinks this is a good idea, so obviously it keeps happening in offices all around the world, despite regular articles in business magazines saying that *blamestorming* makes people unhappy and unproductive. However, it probably feels good for the people in charge, who evade blame by encouraging everyone else to pick a scapegoat. So they will probably continue to schedule *blamestorming* meetings.

Since the verbal model on which *blamestorming* was based, 'brainstorming', is now passé (see THOUGHT SHOWER), we might need a new term for *blamestorming* too. I know – let's have a *fault shower*.

~

bleeding edge

It used to be that exciting new things were 'cutting edge'. Originally this phrase, from the mid-nineteenth century, referred metaphorically to the sharp or incisive nature of a judgement or desire; later it also became possible to be 'at the cutting edge' of some field of endeavour, and for innovative technologies or practices to be called 'cutting edge'. But in the dynamic modern office, it seems 'cutting edge' is no longer, um, cutting-edge enough. The blade has been blunted. If you try to shave with it you'll probably cut your face. Then your face will be bleeding all over the . . . Wait, I've got it! *Bleeding edge!* That sounds so much more exciting, right?

Sadly I have no scientific proof to back up this story about the transformation of 'cutting edge' into *bleeding edge*, but I'm sure you agree it must be true. Pedants, I suppose, could point out the prior use of *bleeding edge* in map-making: according to a 1966 cartographical glossary, the *bleeding edge* is 'an edge of a map to which printed detail extends after the paper has been trimmed' – so perhaps the business adoption, during the shiny and shoulder-padded 1980s, implies pushing boundaries. There is also a sense of 'bleed' that means 'to lose money', so if you are on the *bleeding edge* of some field, perhaps you stand to see your investment evaporate. Since the phrase was initially most popular in descriptions of the computer industry, that sounds about right. (Thomas Pynchon's new novel of the dotcom boom is titled *Bleeding Edge.*)

In any case, these days *bleeding edge* is everywhere, even though few people using it are risking massive plasma loss. Perhaps adopters are subconsciously trying to borrow the glamour of television ER doctors. And maybe people who hear it all the time feel as though they are trapped in a torture-porn movie on constant ketchup-gushing loop.

~

bluegrouping

Bluegrouping is a creative method in which happy office workers re-enact performances by the Blue Man Group, a theatrical collective that puts on shows featuring men with blue faces. New ideas for improving profitability inevitably arise.

That's not really true; in fact *bluegrouping* is a TEAM-building exercise in which workers are bussed out to a nearby forest in order to re-enact ancient Celtic battles with their naked bodies smeared all over in woad.

Or could *bluegrouping* actually be, with depressing predictability, the habit of gathering employees and encouraging them to perform some BLUE-SKY THINKING? I am very much afraid that it could.

~

blue-sky thinking

A blue sky is one with no opaque objects such as clouds in
it. It is perfectly vacant. So *blue-sky thinking* must be the kind
of completely empty thinking unsullied by any ideas at all.

Funnily enough, the earliest recorded metaphorical
uses of the adjectival phrase *blue-sky* were applied to issues
of corporate fraud. In the first years of the twentieth
century, people trading in worthless securities – the kind
of thing that much later would have been termed 'junk
bonds' – were said to be selling 'blue sky and hot air', or
they were called 'blue-sky merchants'. And there is a 1911
reference to an American 'blue sky law', which was
'aimed . . . at corporations which had nothing back of
them but the blue sky'.

The *OED*'s first citation for the modern positive application of *blue-sky* is a 1954 reference to 'blue sky ideas',
attached to a warning that 'unless you can make money on
them, there isn't a chance in the world of you getting
anywhere with them'. Since then, that is what *blue-sky
research* has been understood to mean in the world of
science and technology R&D: it is 'pure' research with no
immediate commercial application.

If, however, a modern worker is told by her boss that
some *blue-sky thinking* is needed, it's probably not the case
that what is wanted is a beautiful piece of obscure pure

mathematics, or a drawing of a space elevator impossible to build with modern technology. No, the demand for *blue-sky thinking* is usually just a highly irritating way of trying to extort a functionally directed 'creativity' from the employee, while simultaneously implying (as with THINKING OUTSIDE THE BOX) that, the rest of the time, her thinking is boring and conventional. Spurred by this example, I am currently working on what will surely be a bestselling book of management theory entitled *Motivate Your Workers with Thinly Veiled Insults*.

~

boil the ocean

We don't want to *boil the ocean* here. Say what? Of course we don't, because that would kill all the fish. (Though to be fair they would then be ready-cooked.) Also it would make a DEEP DIVE pretty uncomfortable.

In a business context, *boiling the ocean* can, strangely, be either good or bad. When it's bad, it just means you're wasting time on an unnecessary inflation of tasks. The thinking is that *boiling the ocean* – though not literally impossible – would take a very long time. And it would. Because a) the ocean is many times bigger than your average kettle; and b) water has a high specific heat capacity, which means you have to put a lot of energy into it to make it boil. The science behind this piece of office jargon is impeccable. The finance website Investopedia offers an example: 'A manager might be accused of trying to *boil the ocean* if he directed his employees to prepare a presentation for a business client based in Houston, Texas, and he insisted that the employees prepare versions of the presentation in Spanish, French, Japanese, Chinese and Italian, just in case someone at the presentation spoke a different language when most likely they would all speak English.'

On the other hand, sometimes *boiling the ocean* is good – confusingly, for exactly the same reason: you are attempting something very difficult and time-consuming, which can be a fine and heroic thing to do. So a company's *boil-the-ocean* STRATEGY – a very ambitious, all-or-nothing approach – could be criticized or praised by onlookers depending on how likely they think it is to succeed. In consulting, meanwhile, a *boil-the-ocean approach* means harvesting all the available data to get at one concentrated truth. (*'Boiling the ocean* to get one cup of hot water.') Though can you imagine all the steam? We wouldn't be able to see a thing.

An early appearance of the phrase *boil the ocean* occurs in an epic 1863 poem of geologically inspired doggerel called *The Earth's Crust; or, Primogenial Scenes,* by one James Lawson. ('Why *boil the ocean,* why forsake her bed? . . . These were, because th'Almighty gave command.') But its modern popularity seems to have been inspired by a famous Second World War exchange between the American actor and comedian Will Rogers and an admiral of the US Navy. Rogers invited the admiral to tell him what his biggest military problem was: maybe he could help. The biggest menace, the admiral said, was the Nazi U-boats. 'Well, that's easy,' Rogers replied. 'You know it's a known fact that submarines can't operate in boiling water. Now it's my suggestion that we boil the ocean.'

'Will,' the admiral said, 'that is a splendid idea, but tell us how you propose to boil the ocean.'

'Admiral,' Rogers replied, 'I am merely giving you the general idea. You will have to fill in the details.'

An inspiration for managers everywhere.

~

bottom out

'I think we need to *bottom* this one *out* at the next meeting.'
Er, what? *Bottoming something out* is not, as innocent souls
might suspect, something people do in the porcelain
privacy of a BIO-BREAK. Instead it means something like 'to
ride out the storm', after the more common intransitive
use of *bottoming out*: when the housing market *bottoms out*,
the only way it can go is up. Thus, to *bottom something out* is
to endure the lowest point of some tricky process or
transition. So, perhaps, to make it through the worst of a
period of explosive gastric distress is to *bottom out* the
bottoming out.

One delightful example is provided by a *Guardian*
reader: 'I got a genuine email from a project manager at
the uni I work at telling us the next few months would be
devoted to "*bottoming out* the roll-out plan, moving going
forward" – verbatim quote there. Showed my boss, he
laughed, now when he asks me to do something he often
adds, "And while you're there, could you *bottom out* the
roll-out plan?"

'PS the project flopped and cost the uni tens of thousands and a good few contracts.'

Bottoms up!

~

breakout area

The *breakout area*, as the name suggests, is a place in the office where you can play the classic 1976 Atari arcade game *Breakout*. In this game, you use a bat to bounce a ball against a wall of bricks at the top of the screen. This is an excellent metaphor for office life. As you destroy bricks – providing a persuasive illusion of progress – the ball speeds up and your bat gets smaller. If your reflexes are sharp enough and you don't miss the ball, you can eventually destroy the whole wall. In this moment, you can dream of escape, to a life of freedom from wage slavery. But escape is not possible, because very soon the wall you have destroyed is replaced – by another wall. In *Breakout*, there are only two walls; in real life, of course, they just keep coming until your inevitable extinction. Calling the part of your workplace prison where you get to play this demotivational metaphor a *breakout area* is, of course, only rubbing it in.

Luckier employees are sometimes encouraged to form *breakout groups*, in which they all play *Breakout* to remind them of the misery and futility of their existence, but in a place outside the office. At least a local bar might provide something to take the edge off.

~

brown-bag session

A *brown-bag session* is when employees take a packed lunch into a meeting. Arguably it would be better used for the more common kind of meeting in which everyone experiences a powerful urge to vomit.

~

bucket

In consulting lingo, *buckets* are just categories. You can also *bucket* or even *bucketize* things, by sorting them into categories. And so office organization is pictured as another infantile children's game of bunging stuff into brightly coloured plastic containers.

You can even – but please don't – say that you have a *time bucket* for some activity. (Try removing the indefinite article and the word *bucket*, and see whether it still makes sense. You, er, 'have time' for something. Yep!) What kind of *bucket* can capture time, and what it means metaphysically for a *time bucket* to fill up or empty, are questions best left to philosophers and Time Lords.

This usage comes from software engineering, where *buckets* are empty documents into which unstructured information is dumped as necessary. But confusingly, *bucketing* is also a form of financial fraud, in which a broker confirms an order to his client without actually executing it yet, hoping to profit from a price change in the meantime. Unscrupulous outfits who do this are known familiarly as *bucket shops*. So we should probably be just as wary of managers who speak too often about *buckets* as we are of cold-calling stock-hawkers.

The fey office use of *bucket* should be discouraged by using it as an inoffensive replacement for the well-known cry of annoyance with which it rhymes. So, several times a day, whenever something goes wrong, shout as loudly as you can: *Bucket!*

~

capacity

A kindly editor asked me just the other day whether I had *capacity* to write a certain article by a certain date. Do I have *capacity*? What, do I look like a container ship? Is ability now to be equated with sheer volume? Do thinner or shorter people have less *capacity*?

Alternatively, *capacity* can be used to describe someone's ability to 'take on board' more information or work. Here I like to imagine a worker screaming silently: 'Why are you trying, as this use of *capacity* implies, actually to insert something into me, while pretending you're being polite by checking first whether there's space among my vital organs and viscera? Isn't that a bit revoltingly invasive?'

Such metaphorical senses of *capacity* have been around a long time; as the *OED* defines it, *capacity* can be 'Mental or intellectual receiving power; ability to grasp or take in impressions, ideas, knowledge'. But this meaning, when used in the workplace context of someone wanting to check your *capacity*, still pictures the unfortunate owner of the questionable *capacity* as an uncomplainingly passive container for whatever info-jism is in the offing.

A crucial office pastime, of course, is *capacity-building*, which means deliberately stretching your stomach bit by bit, through the simple expedient of swallowing more and more bullshit.

~

cascade

To *cascade* something *down* – as opposed to up, where cascades sometimes point? – is to impart information to one's inferiors, in a kind of data-rich golden shower. (As one sceptical internaut relates: 'The first time I heard it I thought, What the fuck, they want me to piss on my TEAM?') In simpler language, *cascade this down* just means pass it on. As a transitive verb, *cascade* derives from twentieth-century electrical physics, where one may *cascade* circuits, which means connecting them in series. But perhaps more germane to the modern office meaning is the older use of *cascade* as navy slang for 'vomit'.

If you want to be a real office-speak ninja, you should try at every opportunity to use the jargon double-whammy of *cascade the learnings*, which I initially thought I had invented as a piss-take but which, gruesomely, is in actual use. The managing director of an Indian sports-wear company says: 'Leadership must percolate down and every mentor I coach should then *cascade the learn-ings* throughout the organization.' Meanwhile, the jolly assistant director of a leadership training programme for students in the Philippines explains: 'Through our student leaders, we aim to *cascade the learnings* to other students as well.' Please think happy thoughts of all these

students arranged atop one another's shoulders like a
wobbly fountain of champagne glasses, and do not ask
precisely what is *cascading* between them.

~

change management

When your company is going through a period of change, you need a special kind of management. What kind of management? *Change management.* The phrase originated in the mid-1960s in studies of business sociology, but gradually *change management* became a business unto itself. In the 1980s, the big six consulting and accountancy companies rebranded their 're-engineering' offerings as *change management services.* These are for when there really are large alterations being made to the company's structure. But now you can't swing a stick without hitting people claiming to be experts in *managing change.* (Naturally, this will often take the form of 'cost leadership', TRANSITIONING, RESIZING, RIGHTSHORING and other euphemisms for sacking people.) And the bloated discipline of *change management* now covers the management of almost every imaginable change, including changes of MISSION, STRATEGY, technology, and structure.

So if we experimentally lop the first word off *change management,* will anything actually be lost? Is *change management* really a genuinely separate species of management worth the name? Is there any such thing as a business where nothing ever changes and so *change management* is unnecessary? Aren't things always changing, and so isn't *change management* just . . . management?

~

checkpoint

The absurdist assault-course that is the modern office now includes *checkpoints*, which are not to be confused with PAIN POINTS, though they may amount to the same thing. A *checkpoint*, according to a 1940 dictionary of aviation, is 'a geographical location on the surface of the land or water, above which the position of an aircraft in flight can be accurately determined by means of visual reference'. The word then acquired the more familiar military meaning of a place where the flow of people or traffic is halted for inspection, as in the famous Checkpoint Charlie at the Berlin Wall.

So what is a *checkpoint* in the office? It's just another happy get-together, or, as analyst and manager Emma Sheldrick defines it, 'a TEAM meeting of some description where the ACTIONS, RISKS and ISSUES are discussed'. No doubt it makes the prospect of the meeting immensely more exciting if everyone imagines themselves as Cold War spies mouthing ambiguously cynical utterances at one another, as in a John le Carré novel.

I note idly that for people who enjoy playing video-games, the primary feeling aroused by a *checkpoint* these days is one of relief, because when you pass a *checkpoint* in a game, that means the system has saved your progress and will automatically restart from there if you get shot in the face. If an office *checkpoint* afforded as much emotional solace, it would have to be redefined as the exact time you leave to go home.

~

circle back

I'm not going to 'get back' to you. That kind of promise
would be a hostage to fortune, implying that I'm soon
going to reply. No; what I'm going to do is *circle back*. I'm
going to go for a long round walk in an enormous field,
and I'm not telling you how big the diameter of the circle
is. It could be miles, like a crop circle made by gargantuan
aliens. Anyway, at some point in the future (I am aggres-
sively leaving this indefinite), I will have come full circle
and be back standing at the place where I started, holding
a basket full of daisies. Will you hear from me then? Not
necessarily. I might have decided in the meantime to *circle
back* to you using a chain of intermediaries, in an amusing
office game of Chinese Whispers.

The point of all this circling is a) to make you feel
dizzy and sick as you contemplate my futile circumambu-
lation; and b) to make myself seem too important and
sophisticated to go in a straight line like humdrum folk,
instead circling like an animal, by which I mean a cool
predator beast (e.g. panther) and not a badger whose
legs are slightly shorter on one side of its body than on
the other.

Just as with the office use of AROUND, *circling back* is also a
passive-aggressive avoidance strategy. When people can't be
bothered to make a decision, rather than actually saying

they can't be bothered they instead suggest that everyone *circle back* to it later. And so the herd trudges on and around in its fatuous rotating conga-line of doom.

~

close of play

The curious strain of kiddy-talk in bureaucratese perhaps
stems from a hope that infantilized workers are more
docile. A manager who tells you to do something *by end of
play* or *by close of play* – in other words, today – is trying to
hypnotize you into thinking you are having fun. This is not
a sodding game of cricket. Though actually, it appears that
the phrase originates from the genteel confines of the
British Civil Service, when there might well have been
cricket, or at least a very long lunch, on the day's agenda of
ACTIONABLES.

Synonymous with asking for something by *close of play* is
requesting it by *end of day*, which is at least less patronizing
in that it doesn't pretend that business hours are filled with
nothing but ludic japes. It still leaves room, however, for
one to wonder: end of *whose* day, exactly? Perhaps the boss
is swanning off at 3 p.m. while everyone else will have to
stay till eight in order to get it done. A day can be an
awfully long time in office politics.

~

cognizant

This little word accomplishes quite a bit. If a boss says 'I'm very *cognizant* that this will mean longer hours', he's saying: a) I'm the kind of smart guy who uses the fancy word *cognizant* when the plebs would just say 'I know that . . .'; but also b) I'm using *cognizant* as a kind of apologetic code-word, because actually apologizing would look weak, so please take this as an unstated apology, but not too much of one, because c) talking about how *cognizant* I am means that all I really care about is my own feelings, and everyone else needs to understand the complexities of my own emotions, and in the meantime they will just have to work longer hours and shut up about it.

~

cold-eye review

A *cold-eye review* could be one of many things. Perhaps a vampire is frostily reconsidering your prospects as his next liquid meal. (Since vampires are dead, their eyes, as well as all their other body parts, are very cold.) Or perhaps I am a restaurant critic, giving my gastronomic opinion of a starter that consists of the ocular organs of a pig, unwarmed: that, too, will be a *cold-eye review*.

In business, however, a *cold-eye review* is just when some-one has a look at your business (or a particular part of it) who is not already familiar with how it works. So the use of *cold* here mixes the familiar senses of 'not prepared' (as in going off *cold-cocked*) and 'unemotional, not invested' (you're as *cold* as ice). It also sounds, well, cool. People with *cold eyes* are assassins, masters of efficiency, spies with licences to kill.

One oil-industry service company, the Impact Response Group, advertises its own *cold-eye review* offering thus: 'The IRG Cold Eye Review will analyze off-target performance and employs Subject Matter Experts to subject our findings to an objective review using the Critical Success Factors model (Leadership, Processes, and Relentless Pursuit).' I must admit that *relentless pursuit* makes me slightly nervous, but 'IMPACT response' is nothing if not a life-or-death business.

If a *cold eye* is useful to get a SENSE CHECK on your STRATEGY, then surely other body parts can get in on the act. My new consulting practice will offer a *hot-tongue review* to brewers of refreshing beer, and – thanks to our highly trained squad of canine assets – a *wet-nose review* for terrified postal workers.

~

collateral

'Distressingly,' reports one *Guardian* reader, 'I was at a meeting recently between two marketing types, one of whom asked the other for the *collateral*. What she meant was the copy for leaflets, posters etc. I despaired inwardly.'

Although *collateral* by itself ought to be a perfectly inoffensive word – it just means something that goes with or accompanies something else, from the Latin for 'together' and 'side' – it probably distresses the sensitive modern office worker because of its ready association in our age with the political euphemism *collateral damage*. As I wrote about that phrase in *Unspeak*:

> To call the killing of human beings 'damage' is to deny their personhood, their existence as individuals, and their crucial difference from inanimate matter. Meanwhile, 'collateral' makes us think of something happening on the sidelines, in the wings: as it were, offstage. The phrase *collateral damage* thus graphically performs its own function: it evokes an image of hiddenness, exactly as its purpose is to hide the reality of what it refers to.

Given the inevitable mental connection to such bloody affairs, then, the office use of *collateral* probably ought to be terminated with extreme prejudice.

~

come to Jesus moment

A *come to Jesus moment* is not to be confused with a *come on Jesus moment* (when you excitedly shout 'Come on, Jesus!' while reading the Gospels), or a *come with Jesus moment* (see *The Exorcist*). In business it means, basically, a moment of truth, when it's time to put up or shut up – or perhaps, as the more coprophiliac vernacular has it, time to shit or get off the pot.

From its melodramatically evangelical tone, you will rightly suspect that the phrase is American in origin, though a British friend of mine who works for a Japanese company recently heard it and was amazed, so it seems to be creeping slowly around the globe. *Forbes* crowned the phrase the winner of its 2013 Jargon Madness contest, explaining that it usually means a confrontation between manager and employee, as in: 'If Joe doesn't improve his productivity, he and I are going to have a *Come To Jesus Moment*.' Strange. So the correct way to handle a poorly performing worker is, what – to wash his feet?

~

competencies

Competency is an old word which has enjoyed a variety of different meanings. From the turn of the seventeenth century it could mean 'competition' or 'sufficiency', or the quality of being legally competent (e.g. as a witness). And it has been used occasionally as a synonym of 'competence', as today, since 1800. So it's one of those apparently modern barbarisms that have a surprisingly long history.

It's only in modern business-talk, however, that it has become popular (or rather, unpopular but ubiquitous). Its rate of use shoots up from 1990, alarmingly like the graph of global temperature. Perhaps *competencies* has displaced 'abilities' because of a perceived rhetorical slight to people with disabilities. And perhaps it has replaced 'skills' because that just sounds too elitist. (Look out for UPSKILL to become *upcompetency*.) One defender of the word *competency* argues: 'It's much broader than "skill". It is something that qualifies you to take on a task. It can be a behaviour, experience, skill, etc.' A sceptic might reply that, if a 'behaviour' or some particular 'experience' really qualifies you for a task, it must be because it has given you some extra *skill* that helps you do the work.

Whatever our view of the necessity of the word, it is definitely true these days that only if you have the *core competencies* will you be able to ACTION the KEY DELIVERABLES for your relevant STAKEHOLDERS, GOING FORWARD.

Management professor Bruce Barry doesn't like *core competencies*, though. As he told *Forbes*: 'Do people talk about peripheral competency? Being competent is not the standard we're seeking. It's like core mediocrity.'

Such is the brutal competitiveness of the workplace, even *core competencies* might not be enough. People actually talk all the time about KEY *core competencies*. (So as, presumably, to distinguish them from *dispensable peripheral competencies*.) I myself enjoy an impressive range of *crucial* KEY *core competencies*, chief among which is the ability to spot ridiculous tautologies.

~

creative abrasion

Creative abrasion means using sandpaper to obtain an interesting variety of surface textures in your artwork. All right, no, it doesn't – it's just a peculiarly icky term for managing a TEAM of people with different thinking and working styles. The phrase seems to have been invented by Dorothy Leonard and Susaan Straus, who explained their theory in a 1997 article for *Harvard Business Review.* 'The manager successful at fostering innovation figures out how to get different approaches to grate against one another in a productive process we call *creative abrasion.*'

To *grate against one another?* That sounds potentially painful. An article in *Bloomberg BusinessWeek* takes a more pleasant-sounding approach to the theme of surface friction, explaining that *creative abrasion* is necessary because 'you have to make the different approaches rub together in productive ways'. It's true that people in offices *rub together* quite often, though usually out of sight of the bosses, especially if there is a strict company policy about employee romance. But when happy rubbing-together becomes actual *abrasion* – which means 'scraping', 'grazing', 'shaving off' – you might end up wanting some antiseptic cream and strategically placed Band-Aids.

~

crossumer

A *crossumer* is not, as might seem initially appropriate, a consumer who is really cross – perhaps because your company's products are deficient. The word seems to come from the world of Spanish marketing English, which also likes to speak of *fansumers* (consumers who like your product), *prosumers* (consumers who use your product really hard, or 'professionally'), and even *persumers*. (A *persumer* is a mixture of consumer and person. Unlike all those other consumers who are, I don't know, bees and rocks.)

Anyway, in this brave new world of prefixing anything you like to *-sumer*, a *crossumer* is a consumer who is adept at using internet services and shares experiences on social media. In other words, a *crossumer* is a customer who uses Twitter. But beware: since many celebrities on Twitter like to exploit their bully-pulpit and bore the pants off their followers by ranting about bad customer service from a telephone company or at an airport, some *crossumers* might actually be very cross after all.

~

deadlined

In alarmed confidence, an editor reports a troubling new verbing: 'I *deadlined* this for Friday.' Seriously? Well, there's no stopping it now. A particular virtuoso of using *deadline* as a verb is the media and journalism professor Charles Warner, who advises us to 'Set goals (always time framed – *deadlined*).' He also wants to know: 'Did the team leader clearly articulate the team's goals (which should have been reasonable and *deadlined*)?', and warns us: 'To-Do lists that contain a large number of things you intend to accomplish are virtually useless unless they are prioritized and *deadlined*.' (I heartily agree, which is why I gave up making to-do lists altogether.)

Although office jargonistas might not be aware of it, the word *deadline* is itself originally a military borrowing. In the mid-nineteenth century it meant 'A line drawn around a military prison, beyond which a prisoner is liable to be shot down'. And *deadlined* is still American military jargon: vehicles that are *deadlined* are those that are broken down or extremely unsafe. So, that *deadlined* project? Wouldn't go near it if I were you.

~

deep dive

Deep dive is one of the many office metaphors that attempt
to make paper-shuffling sound more like an exotically
adventurous sport. Workers are not expected actually to
strap on scuba gear in preparation for a *deep dive*, which just
means getting into the details, i.e. going GRANULAR, or
indeed DRILLING DOWN. But *deep dive* makes you sound like a
cross between Jacques Cousteau (or indeed Steve Zissou)
and James Bond, with a wetsuit on over his tuxedo, silently
infiltrating a supervillain's underwater nuclear facility.

An early use of *deep dive* to mean something other than
profound aquatic submersion comes in a nineteenth-
century magazine story, 'Stronger than Death', by M.
Campbell: '"By the way, I found his first letter, the one that
you wanted to look at; I believe I've got it in my pocket
now." And papa made a *deep dive*, and brought a letter to
light.' (Spoiler: it wasn't the right letter.) But the world
didn't have to wait long for a glimmer of the modern use of
deep dive as 'a detailed look': it is already there in a certain
Mrs Gerald Paget's 1908 treatise on society's unfair atti-
tudes to women, *Going Through the Mill*, where Chapter 12
is excitingly introduced thus: 'THE CHRONICLER TAKES
A DEEP DIVE INTO CAUSES, AND COMES INTO
VIOLENT COLLISION WITH AN EFFECT.'

By now *deep-diving* is so common in office parlance that

it's a wonder people get any time to dry off. You can take a *technical deep dive*, or a *leadership deep dive*, or a *deep dive into business intelligence* (which, like military intelligence, is sometimes said to be a contradiction in terms). One unimprovably soporific book title says it all: *Deep Dive: The Proven Method for Building Strategy* . . . (the title goes on but I lost all awareness before reaching the end). Rather belatedly, a Harvard Business School paper from 2010 claims to 'introduce the concept of a *deep dive*', though it had already been around for a long time. Perhaps the authors mean something slightly different. See if you can tell from their definition: a *deep dive*, they say, is 'an intervention when top management seizes hold of the substantive content of a strategic initiative and its operational implementation at the project level, as a way to drive new behaviours that enable an organization to shift its performance trajectory into new dimensions unreachable with any of the previously described forms of intervention.' No? Me neither.

In a 2008 'leadership' handbook, most disturbingly of all, we even read of subjecting employees to *deep-dive interviews*. The idea of conducting a deep dive *inside another person* is about as disgustingly intrusive as modern office jargon gets.

Those promised that a *deep dive* is coming up could do worse than follow the kindly instructions offered in 1870 by a magazine article on diving: 'I have found it a good preparation for a deep dive to inhale a few draughts of fresh air just previously, expelling it forcibly each time, in order to fill the lungs with a wholly pure supply.' If everyone in the office did this each time *deep dive* were mentioned, adding the bulging eyes and cheek-puffing common to goldfish impersonations, so that all were engaged in a simultaneous pantomime of fishy heavy breathing, perhaps the term could thereby be mocked into obscurity.

~

define the North Star

To *define the North Star* is to tell an inspiring story about the company's aims, and what world-shattering consequences their fulfilment will have. Some observers blame this phrase on Coca-Cola, which in early 2013 released some marketing guff – sorry, a marketing MISSION statement – which explained: 'We need to define the North Star, some big audacious IMPACT on popular culture.' (This was, apparently, because we now live in a 'new liquid world', which presumably isn't a world totally dissolved in the acidy sweetness of Coca-Cola, nor a sly reference to the philosopher Zygmunt Bauman's notion of 'liquid modernity'.)

But *defining the North Star* predates this info-bomb. In a set of slides from an American public-research institute dated 2010, we are encouraged to 'Define the "North Star" – what RESULT makes all this effort worthwhile?' Pursuing the navigational theme even further, the writer then exhorts us to 'Define the "ship" – what resources do we have? What do we need? (time, funds, expertise)'. My ship is the ship of Theseus, all the parts of which have been replaced so that philosophers can wrangle for ever about whether it is still the same ship. Or maybe it is the ship of fools. (These slides are written in the world's stupidest font, Comic Sans, so that seems quite likely.)

One telecommunications blogger, meanwhile, uses

defining the North Star in a splendidly jargon-dense context: 'Industry, regulatory and standardization bodies need to collaborate more tightly and define the North Star vision and benefits derived as a result of harmonized LTE spectrum and then make the interim tough choices and decisions to get there.' Got that?

The only problem with all this creative stargazing is that the North Star is already permanently defined as being Polaris. You can't just unilaterally redefine it as being something else. Or you'll get irretrievably lost, like the willowy heroine of a Haruki Murakami novel.

~

deliverables

To say that you are *delivering* (e.g. 'results') sounds nice and dynamic, as well as concretely physical, as though space were being traversed in order to give someone an important package. The connotations of a postal service can even be positively heroic, as we all know from admiring the post-apocalyptic mail-work of Kevin Costner in the deathless blockbuster *The Postman*.

Inevitably, as with the construction ACTIONABLES, we also now have *deliverables*. ('KEY deliverables,' Don Watson notes thoughtfully, 'are the most important ones.') According to the *OED*, *deliverables* as 'a tangible result of a development process' originated in computer-speak in the late 1980s, and then rapidly spread out from IT into the wider world of work.

A characteristically depressing job advert from 2000 reads: 'As well as assessing the effectiveness of programme *deliverables*, you will also be responsible for all RISK MANAGEMENT.' Meanwhile, in 2002, the in-house magazine of the US Army wrote wistfully: 'The Army . . . must also struggle against perceptions among propensed and non-propensed youth that . . . [it] provides the least attractive cultural, technical, and economic "*deliverables*".'

I do admire the writer's elegant tossing-off of the pleasantly obscure 'propensed' to mean inclined or disposed to join the army in the first place, but it's a shame that the army is thought to provide the least attractive *deliverables*. Mind you, that's not surprising when you consider being on the other end of the kind of *deliverables* that come at you very fast from an artillery piece or a rocket launcher.

~

demising

In April 2013 HSBC announced that it was sacking 3,000 people. Of course, it didn't say that; it said it was *demising* their roles. The *Guardian* reported this banking euphemism thus: 'The bank is getting rid of more than 3,000 jobs, and it doesn't even have the decency to use plain English.' Plain it might not be, but *demising* is – or at least used to be – English. The *OED* records an 'obsolete' sense of *demise* meaning 'to let go: to dismiss' that dates at least from 1541. To rejuvenate an old meaning of a word is arguably quite a nice thing to do – or at least it would be were the intention not to cloak disposal in the garb of poetry.

But there has long been an irreconcilable confusion between two senses of *demise*. It is often popularly used to mean 'downfall', though for most of its history it has strictly meant 'death' (the original legal meaning is the transfer of an estate by will or lease). So HSBC's admirable lexical archaeology might not catch on, since it could sound too awkwardly murderous. No company really wants to acquire the reputation of one that actually kills its employees.

~

diarize

This verb, hideous to some, used to mean something quite pleasant and literary: to write regularly in one's diary, keeping a record of each day's experiences. ('Dear diary, here are the gory visions of megaviolence that assailed me at work today . . .') Now, however, it's used to mean 'find time in our respective schedules' ('Let's *diarize*!'), or just 'schedule' ('I *diarized* it for Monday'). Slightly cleverer is the organizational practice of *diarization* in law firms and elsewhere: this means that a file is marked to be looked up again at a certain date, in case anything needs to be done about it.

There's nothing wrong, of course, with economizing on words: *diarize* is so much more efficient than 'put in the diary'. But who actually uses diaries any more? Scheduling systems these days are usually electronic, and they're almost all called calendars. Hence one can also say *calendarize* – that is, if one cares nothing at all for verbal aesthetics. In his jargon guide *Shoot the Puppy*, Tony Thorne notes that the continued use of 'pencil you in' is inconsistent with digitized diarization. 'I'll enter you (in) seems set to replace it,' he writes, 'and a nuance of difference may be lost.' The feeling of tentativeness may well be lost, but a new connotation is added. I'll *enter you*. I'll *enter you in*. And so is born another horrible way (see also CAPACITY, DEEP-DIVE INTERVIEW) of portraying the subordinate as the recipient of unwanted PENETRATION.

~

dipstick

Particularly common in Indian business English is the
idea of a *dipstick test* or a *dipstick survey*, leading to *dipstick
results*. In spring 2013 a new Hindi entertainment TV
channel was announced, reported the *Times of India*,
after 'a *dipstick test* found that there was a market' for it.
Of course, *dipstick results* are also the indicators produced
by the most common urine-analysis test, but Indian
businessmen are not literally pissing on their customers.
Nor are they secretly smuggling urine-testing devices
into millions of homes. They are merely, let us say,
testing the waters.

Some international confusion is bound to arise here.
An American contributor to *Forbes* tells the unhappy story
of 'working for dipstick owners, doing dipstick things in
the dipstick way they wanted them done because I needed
the work and wanted to keep the job, and signing off on
the *dipstick results* that I got for doing the dipstick things'.
Here, *dipstick results* are not those of a rough-and-ready
market survey or microbiological analysis of urine, but just
the kind of results you would expect from doing dipstick
things mandated by dipstick owners, in other words
dipsticks, or idiots.

The moral of all this is that you should be careful not to
do a *dipstick test* if that means consulting only complete

morons about your business plan. In that case you might as well flush the *dipstick results* straight down the pan on your next BIO-BREAK.

~

dogfooding

Dogfooding is the newer way to say *eating your own dogfood*, because who has time to say four words when they could turn another noun into a verb? We all know that eating our own dogfood is a good idea. Because – wait, we're *dogs*? We're a yapping little cluster of puppies who should eat our own dogfood rather than steal the dogfood belonging to the rival pack next door? What is this?

Actually, it's even weirder than that, because we dogs apparently cooked our own dogfood in the first place. That's why we should eat it. An entrepreneurial mutt would presumably look into creating a dogfood delivery start-up to service all the nation's hounds. But if he doesn't eat his own dogfood, he won't have reliable quality control.

The phrase originates with an internal Microsoft email in 1988 with the subject line 'Eating our own Dogfood', in which one manager told another that they should be using their own server software within the company. So *eating your own dogfood*, or *dogfooding*, means using the product you are hoping to sell to other people.

Fine, but it's still a mystery quite where the dogs come in. It seems improbable that the Microsoft guy was trying to imply either that everyone working at Redmond was a four-legged canine (or at a pinch a werewolf), or that their own products were so bad that they tasted like dogfood does to humans, i.e. like crap, and so using them was just supposed to be a form of masochistic self-punishment. Wouldn't it be more optimistic and on-trend to say *eating our own cupcakes?*

~

double-loop learning

Double-loop learning is what happens when a child tries to understand how to tie her shoelaces. Obviously it's gradually being phased out of the modern world thanks to convenient Velcro fasteners on tiny trainers. But the resurgence of interest in handicrafts allows us to hope that *double-loop learning* will at least live on among the quiet but powerful global army of knitters.

Things are a bit more athletic in the corporate world. '*Double-loop learning* is built into many agile processes, most notably Scrum, and is also the objective of the lessons learned process prescribed by the Project Management Institute Project Management Body of Knowledge,' explains one consulting firm. None the wiser? Well, according to a 1977 article in *Harvard Business Review* that introduced the phrase, *double-loop learning* is when you fail to achieve a goal a few times and then decide that maybe you should change the goal a little bit, or even abandon it. It is thus better than *single-loop learning*, which is making repeated, failed attempts to achieve a goal without changing one's method or wondering whether the goal is in fact worth having. In other words, *double-loop learning* is pretty much definable as 'not being a complete idiot'.

In the post-crisis world, however, even not being a complete idiot might not be enough to guarantee success.

And so some bright spark has already announced a superior process called – what else? – *triple-loop learning*. According to Authentic Leadership International, an executive-coaching firm with the glorious slogan 'ALIGNING core values to action for real change', *triple-loop learning* 'involves transforming who we are by creating a shift in our context or point of view about ourselves. It involves "learning how to learn" by reflecting on how we learn in the first place . . . This form of learning helps us to understand a great deal more about ourselves and others regarding beliefs and perceptions. *Triple-loop learning* might be explained as *double-loop learning* about *double-loop learning*.'

Sometimes it's a blessing to be completely out of the loop.

~

download

So as to sound more sexily technical – even if they are barely able to operate Excel – more and more people are adopting the term *download* to mean 'impart information' or, basically, 'talk'. One *Guardian* commenter, for example, complains bitterly of a manager who regularly says: 'I'm going to *download* to you about our last meeting.' This adoption of an IT term is particularly brutalizing, of course, since it pictures the poor subordinate as a mere storage device, a virgin hard drive of sufficient CAPACITY to faithfully copy down all the nonsense that is being streamed to it. It also reinforces the vertical metaphor of office hierarchy: if I am *downloading* to you, it must be because I am higher than you. Someone who is fed up with being *downloaded* to might dream of taking advantage of the two-way nature of most data pipes by *uploading* a tiny package of malware that would infect and spread among the executives, with the result that they all eventually spoke nothing but gibberish. But then, who would notice?

~

drill down

Far be it from me to suggest that managers prefer
metaphors that evoke huge pieces of phallic machinery,
but why else say *drill down* if you just mean 'look at in
detail'? Like many examples of bureaucratese, *drill down*
has a specific sense in information technology: to
follow the hierarchical ladder of a data-analysis menu
down through to the individual datum. Naturally, when
you clamber back to the chilled atmosphere of a
HELICOPTER VIEW, you are *drilling up*. In accounting software, not only can you *drill down, drill up* and *drill in*,
but you can even *drill around*, much as a disturbingly
incompetent dentist might, or as old-school Texas oil
speculators used to do. To *drill down* or *drill around*,
then, is an IT metaphor rather similar to that of 'data
mining'. (In Australia, 'Drill Down' is the refreshingly
straightforward name for a company that 'offers job
seekers an introduction to what it's like working in the
mines', by which they mean working in actual holes
underground.)

It's probably because *drill down* sounds like such a
devastating display of potency that it then came to be used
in non-technical senses where there is no hierarchical
analysis possible. It has even leaked out into television
news, where anchors will promise to *drill down* into a story,

by which they mean get an attractive reporter to tell you a little more about it while standing in front of a vaguely relevant building.

~

drivers

In Formula One motor racing, the KEY *drivers* are . . . er, the
drivers. The people driving the race-cars the fastest, for lots
of money. In the more sedate world of the office, however,
speedy tyre-turners are not so well compensated. There,
one hears incessantly of 'the KEY *drivers* for change'. Spare a
sympathetic thought for the poor bastards doomed to
circumnavigate a racetrack for just a handful of coins.

Unless I have been grasping the wrong end of the stick
all this time, and the office use of *drivers* doesn't refer to
people piloting automobiles. But in that case it apparently
means literally anything at all – factors, ideas, causes,
'stuff' . . . Happily, *drivers* makes it sound like management
knows where it's going, or at least has turned on the satnav.

~

ducks in a row, get our

'We have to get our *ducks in a row* on this.' Why? What kind of maniac thinks ducks always have to be lined up perfectly in a row? They are birds, wild and free! Let them waddle where they please! Or are we meant to think of a delicious Chinese buffet featuring crispy Peking ducks all lined up for the delectation of all the guests? Or flying duck-sculptures arranged diagonally on the interior wall of a small house in a depressing British television soap opera?

The earliest known printed use of the phrase – meaning to get organized, to have things in place – is from an American newspaper in 1889 ('the Democrats are getting their *ducks in a row*'), but authorities still don't agree on its origin. Some say it derives from the use of ducks to mean pins in American bowling. (So you'd line them up before rolling a huge ball at them.) Another more alarming possibility is that getting your *ducks in a row* literally means lining up living fowls through treacherously placed bait so that you can kill more than one of them with a single blast of your shotgun. But I prefer to think happier thoughts of a mother duck leading her adorably fluffy little ducklings, who follow behind her in single file – perhaps, to be strict, you'd call it more of an undulating line of ineffable cuteness, but let's agree that *row* would also do. Because frankly the alternatives are just too sad.

Once you have got all your *ducks in a row*, watch out for the malign apparition of the *duck shuffler* – someone who messes things up at the last moment. I for one have problems imagining shuffling ducks, because waterfowl are not as conveniently flat as playing cards. So I propose calling this ornery troublemaker a *duck kicker* or perhaps a *duck bandit*.

~

environmental scanning

This sounds a bit like HORIZON SCANNING, except that you are not trying to see so far; instead you are taking a keen and ecologically friendly interest in the flora and fauna immediately surrounding you. The enjoyably geeky use of *scanning* probably means you are using a super-hi-tech tool to do this, like a *Star Trek* tricorder. But your heightened interest in the environment does not, of course, mean you are a keen amateur botanist. As analyst Emma Sheldrick helpfully explains, *environmental scanning* means 'Looking around to see what others are doing, then copying it'. There has to be a BEST PRACTICE somewhere round here, right? Perhaps over there, under that pile of rotting leaves.

~

expectations

Expectations are flexible things, and people will no doubt carry on having them even if the lingo surrounding them is logically complete nonsense. For example, one *Guardian* commenter reports: 'In a team meeting a few months ago, the then manager said "There's no reason that all of you shouldn't get a rating of Exceeds Expectations every review if you all work hard." She didn't like it when I pointed out that if she expected us to exceed expectations, it was then literally impossible for us to do so.' Touché!

It would be good if employees were able to manage the expectations of their managers, but *managing expectations* usually means something more outward-facing and defeatist: preparing your clients or customers psychologically for the inevitable fact that the DELIVERABLES will be rubbish.

If you fail to brainwash your clients – I mean *manage expectations* – successfully, or if you fail to meet the expected grade of 'Exceeds Expectations', then you will have fallen victim to the dreaded *expectation gap*, which is the yawning existential chasm between the satisfaction people hope to derive from their work and the soul-destroying quotidian experience of it.

~

flagpole, run this up the

Let's *run this up the flagpole*! This exhortation to mean 'give it a try' or 'test it' came to prominence in the 1950s Madison Avenue advertising industry. It derived from a yarn that was doing the rounds about the first President, George Washington. When Betsy Ross presented the new American flag to him, he was supposed to have quipped: 'Let's run it up the flagpole and see if anyone salutes it.' The original sense, then – as in minor variations such as 'Let's run it up the flagpole and see if it unfurls' or '. . . and see which way it waves' – was to test something (e.g. an ad campaign) in public or at least in front of the clients, rather than just around the office: a nuance that has since got lost.

Even back then, in any case, let's *run it up the flagpole* was spawning humorous competition: a 1958 issue of *Life* magazine also records Mad Men slang such as 'Let's follow it and see what it eats', and 'Let's get down on all fours and look at it from the client's point of view.' (Either this is supposed to be slightly risqué, encouraging one's colleagues to adopt a doggy-style position, or it implies that the client is an extremely small person or idiotic child.) The annoying ad-man juror in the 1957 film adaptation of *Twelve Angry Men* is amusingly full of them: as well as 'Let's *run it up the flagpole* and see if anyone salutes it', he offers

'Let's throw it out on the stoop and see if the cat licks it up', 'Let's chip up a few shots to see if any of them land on the green', and even the rather charming 'Let's put it on the bus, see if it gets off at Wall Street.'

Later variations on the theme include 'Let's cross the sidewalk and see what the view looks like from over there', or 'Let's put it on the radiator and see if it melts', or even (so I am assured) 'Let's knife-and-fork it and see what comes out.' (Comes out from *where*? That's disgusting.)

There seems no end to the forced jollity (and despair-inducing implied exclamation mark) of such constructions. Let's brown the onions and see if they need any garlic! Let's roll it up into a tube and see if anyone thinks it's a light sabre! Let's smash the boss's head in and see if we get sent to prison!

~

going forward

Top of many people's hate-list is this now-ubiquitous way of
saying 'from now on' or 'in future'. It has the added sly
rhetorical aim of wiping clean the slate of the past (perhaps
because 'mistakes were made'); indeed it is a kind of
incantation or threat aimed at shutting down conversation
about whatever bad thing has happened. *Going forward*
you'll forget about it, if you know what's good for you. This
aspect of the phrase proves to be especially attractive to
politicians, who like to accuse their critics of being mired in
the past. For a democratic leader – perhaps especially a
'progressive' one – every day is a fresh start. Not coinciden-
tally, the official pronouncements of Barack Obama's
administration are littered with *going forward* or its sibling
moving forward, which at the time of writing have been
deployed nearly 600 times in the past year in official White
House transcripts and press releases.

For most of the twentieth century, only particular things
could be said to be *going forward*: people receiving prizes,
litigation, military operations. Surprisingly, the modern
standalone usage does not appear in the archives of *Time*
magazine until 1998, when there is a rash of initial examples such as 'The category killers are going to have to live
with lower profit margins *going forward*' and 'Home sales
will be treated vastly differently *going forward*.'

Going forward helpfully implies a kind of thrustingly strategic progress, and *moving forward* perhaps even more so – even though none is likely to be made as long as the work-day is made up of funereal meetings where people say things like '*going forward*'.

But it does boast the potential for being deployed in ways that are breathtakingly disingenuous. A splendid example came in July 2013, when a spokesman for payday-loan companies was asked on the BBC whether the lenders enquired about customers' existing income and expenditure before making a loan. '*Going forwards* they will,' he said brightly. In other words: No, they don't!

~

granular

Granularity is that uncomfortably scratchy sensation you get at the beach when sand has dried in places it shouldn't. Surfers also love the *granular* because it means rad foam, or whatever they call it. But a *granular* view can be applied to other things besides sandy crevices of intimate flesh or the ideal conditions for standing on a board that is floating in the sea, and you don't need to be staring at grains of wheat either.

The office-speak *granular* originates in computer database talk, and is now widely used to imply a data-savvy, scientific approach, though it usually just means looking at the details. After DRILLING DOWN, you arrive at a *granular* perspective, which is no doubt preferable to finding yourself boiling alive in hot lava.

Getting granular is usually thought to be a virtue for people fiddling with stuff like geographic or purchasing data ('How *granular* can we get on this?' 'Really *granular*!' 'Awesome!'). Confusingly, though, the word can sometimes be used as a complaint; a boss might say that an analysis is too *granular* and instead ask for an 'executive summary'. (In other words, a summary, but one named so that it flatters his ego.) People the world over find *granular* unnecessary and irritating, so all office uses of it should probably be taken with a large quantity of some *granular* condiment.

~

guerrilla edit

A *guerrilla edit* is the euphemism used by armed insurgents for the occasional sad necessity of executing one of their own number. (That's one fewer guerrillas!) In the office saturated with militaristic fantasies, meanwhile, a *guerrilla edit* occurs if – just imagine – you can write your part of a document while other people write their parts. Man, Che Guevara had nothing on Office 365.

~

hands and feet, give it

To *give* something *hands and feet* is to flesh it out (so to speak), to complete it, to fill in the details. This curious little expression is common in Dutch business English, where it constantly irritates an Amsterdamer friend. It also appears in an American college's 2013 MISSION statement, which explains: 'We need to remain passionate about our mission but also flexible and creative about how to embody it. By "embody" I mean how to *give it hands and feet* in the changing world of 21st-century higher education.'

This is a peculiar bunch of metaphors if you stop to think about it too closely. You want to *embody* a MISSION? And you'll do that by giving it hands and feet? What, it doesn't need a torso? The poor thing can do without a head? It's just going to be all hands and feet and nothing else, like a horrible stitched-together monster from the id?

It's possible that *give it hands and feet* snuck into the office lexicon by way of Christian singer-songwriter Rich Mullins, one couplet of whose 1996 song 'Screen Door' goes: 'Faith comes from God and every word that He breathes / He lets you take it to your heart so you can *give it hands and feet*'. (Now I'm picturing *words*, of all things, running around on tiny feet and waving enormous foam hands. Or is it just me?)

Whatever its origin, the phrase *give it hands and feet*

seems to be irritating because of its infantilizing cutesiness, as though working on some tedious project were the equivalent of moulding little men with little fingers and toes out of modelling clay in kindergarten. Perhaps a more modern and grown-up approach would be to say 'Let's give this tits and a cock'?

~

heads-up

'I just wanted to give you a *heads-up* on . . .' is now the correctly breath-wasting way to say 'I just wanted to tell you about . . .'. But what exactly is a *heads-up*? It's spelled like this (not *head's-up*) because the origin, in American engineering and military circles of the early twentieth century, is an exhortation for all the members of your squad or crew (so *heads*, plural) to pay attention because something potentially dangerous is about to happen. They should literally straighten their necks and raise their heads. So the call 'Heads up!' means 'Watch out!'

The 1970s saw the invention of the military technology called a *heads-up display*: crucial information from a fighter jet's instruments was projected on to the cockpit windshield. That way, the pilot did not have to peer down to check a dial but could keep his head up constantly.

So *heads-up* originated in situations where something hairy was about to happen, or where life-or-death information was being provided to an elite warrior. Naturally, neither of those things is ever true when the noun phrase *a heads-up* is used in the modern office. Time, perhaps, for a *heads-down*, when everyone takes a quiet snooze at their desks.

~

helicopter view

Office life is so exciting, with all its DEEP DIVES and helicopter rides! Dully, though, to take a *helicopter view* is not to mow down villagers in a re-enactment of the Vietnam War but simply to look at things on a large scale. 'A course I was imprisoned in,' confides one worker, 'actually gave everyone a little helicopter lapel badge to remember that they needed to do it.' Bastards.

You'll guess that *helicopter view* can't be all that old a phrase, since the first mass-produced modern helicopter, the US military's Sikorsky R4, appeared only in 1944, and the first civilian helicopter (the Bell 47) in 1946. Still, it didn't take long for a literal use of *helicopter view* to appear: in a 1952 issue of *Life* magazine, where the photographer Margaret Bourke-White describes the experience of taking pictures from a helicopter in order to produce what she calls '*Life*'s cross-country *helicopter view* of America'.

That same year, a reference to what seems to be the first metaphorical use of *helicopter view* appears in a rather unlikely place, William A. Spurrier's book *Guide to the Christian Faith: An Introduction to Christian Doctrine*. 'Some moderns,' he writes, 'still believe that it is possible to "get behind" all the interpretations and records and arrive at a clear, objective, and factual picture of the "simple Jesus." This has been labelled, "The *Helicopter View* of Jesus" (Paul

Lehmann). But there is no way to get behind the present evidence.'

Staring at Jesus from a mental chopper is a pleasant image, but this doesn't seem to work in quite the same way as our modern *helicopter view* in office-speak, which just means a wide survey or a bird's-eye view. (Birds, though, are not as tough and exciting as massive thwopping flying machines.) But a year later, in 1953, we find what appears to be the first familiar use, in (of course) the *Proceedings of the Annual Conference of State Mediation Agencies*: 'Where we've seen only the trees, your folks introduced a *helicopter view* of the forest which permitted you to point out the paths toward settlement. I've often wondered and speculated as to how you do it.' Such a wondrous vehicle must be something like the metaphorical Helicopter of Truth mentioned in Lucien Jones's philosophical treatise *The Transparent Head*. This sense grew popular in business parlance over the next years, until a 1969 journal article presents it as an established fact that a good manager needs 'A "*helicopter view*" of the whole business landscape that will prevent him from becoming too obsessed with detail'.

It's true that it's boring to become too obsessed with detail. To avoid the horrors of detail, we need only travel ever further upwards. Replace *helicopter view* with *B-52 view*, then with *International Space Station view*, and then ideally with *Andromeda Galaxy view* – where, at a safe distance of 2.5 million light years, we'll be unable to perceive any detail at all and can breathe the pure vacuum of STRATEGY.

~

hit the ground running

Did it never occur to anyone who uses this phrase that *to hit the ground running* is quite a stupid thing to do? Don't ever attempt such a silly stunt: you should, of course, execute the standardized PLF (Parachute Landing Fall) in order to dissipate the force of hitting the ground. *Then* you can start running. But if you tried to *hit the ground running* you would presumably have to start running while still in mid-air, like Wile E. Coyote with a parachute. Then one of your feet would touch the ground first, taking all the force of your falling body in an almost certainly less-than-optimal position. You would probably break your leg. And then curse the idiot who ever thought it was a good idea to *hit the ground running*.

'But what about parachuting soldiers?' you ask. Well, according to the US Army's 2003 *Field Manual on Static Line Parachuting Techniques and Tactics*, of which we all have a well-thumbed copy, they're not expected to *hit the ground running* either: 'To lessen the possibility of injuries, the parachutist is trained to absorb the impact of landing by executing a proper PLF.' Military commanders do actually use the phrase *to hit the ground running* when talking about paratroopers, but it's not meant strictly literally. The point is just that the troops have to get moving immediately *after* landing.

So the borrowing of this term for office use – to mean, er, 'start quickly' – is another military-fantasy metaphor that seduces workers who like to feel they are soldiering. Perhaps it would become less popular if everyone adopted the alternative proposed etymology offered by the legendary *New York Times* language columnist William Safire, who in a 1981 column suggested that it might derive from 'hobo lingo'. How so? 'I have no citations to support this,' Safire says modestly, 'but it seems to me that when a hobo was stealing a ride on a freight train, and saw a "cinderbull" (railroad detective) approaching, he was tempted to leap from the moving train. In that case, to avoid a bad fall, he would pump his legs in the hope of maintaining balance when he hit the ground, or at least until he could roll into a soft spot.'

Sweet. So next time someone uses *hit the ground running*, you can reply, all innocence: 'What, you mean like a tramp?'

~

holding the ring

Holding the ring is a fraught business, as anyone knows who has been a nervous best man patting the pocket where he is keeping the wedding ring, or anyone who has attempted to grasp a burning ring of fire (it burns burns burns), or indeed anyone who has been Frodo Baggins. In the office, *holding the ring* is a deliberate Tolkien reference: the unfortunate employee who is tasked with carrying the evil gold band – forged in the fires of Mount Doom and known as the One Ring, the Doom of Man, the Ruling Ring, the Master Ring, the Ring of Power, or Isildur's Bane – is sent on a tedious quest with a bunch of not-very-funny dwarves, and feels his soul gradually becoming corrupted.

Originally, *holding the ring* (or *keeping the ring*) comes from the noble art of pugilism: it could mean either watching a series of boxing matches, or being a victorious fighter holding out against all-comers, or keeping order in the ring. It's this last meaning (perhaps also with a hint of the circus-master lording it over the circus-ring) that lends *holding the ring* its (real, I confess) managerial sense: either keeping things trundling along during some set period (perhaps exploiting one's skills in CHANGE MANAGEMENT), or taking overall responsibility for some task: 'I will *hold the ring* on that project.'

Obviously it's only to perverted minds that an invitation to *hold the ring* could sound rather disgustingly intimate. Eww, hold your *own* ring, dude.

~

horizon scanning

Horizon scanning is something you do as the hero of a Western, squinting coolly into the desert distance for signs of the dust thrown up by approaching horses. Thus business types can also cast themselves as photogenic gunslinging frontierspeople by saying they perform *horizon scanning*, when what they really mean is that sometimes they think more than five minutes into the future in order to imagine what might happen next. Here's a helpful example from the British government's Health and Safety Executive: 'HSE undertakes *horizon scanning* and other futures activities to help increase awareness of developments, trends and other potential changes in the world of work.' (*Futures activities* is rather marvellous, isn't it?)

Of course, under certain atmospheric conditions, what you think you see on the horizon can be just a seductive mirage. But never mind that. We are everywhere reassured that *horizon scanning* – which is defined in consulting lingo as part of RISK MANAGEMENT – has apparently long been performed by all kinds of official agencies (government departments, police forces, and so forth), as well as banks and all other corporations worth their salt. It's obviously thanks to this ubiquitous *horizon scanning* that no one is ever surprised by anything and no unforeseen crisis ever occurs.

~

human capital

Capital – in the sense of spare piles of money to be gambled with – makes the world go round, so what better way to show your respect for the people under your employ than by calling them *human capital?* Don't listen to the sandal-wearing Marxists whining that human beings are fleshly individuals with their own hopes and dreams and oughtn't to be considered as a kind of Borg-like financial-ized collective whose only purpose is to breed more capital for the shareholders.

The idea of *human capital* was popularized by economists in the 1960s, but seems to have become widespread in office-talk only since the turn of the millennium. Now it is often seen in close conjunction with *human resources* (HR people nowadays are interested in *human capital management*), though the two phrases have subtly different negative connotations. *Human resources* implies that people are fungible (one easily exchangeable for another), and exist to be put to use, and further that there is basically an infinite supply of them. (The word 'resource' means something that will spring up again.) *Human resources* are like so-called 'natural resources': they are there to be exploited, with no thought to their possible exhaustion.

Human capital, on the other hand, concentrates on the power of people so described to breed more money for you. It does have an ostensibly caring aspect; as Investopedia defines it, part of the idea is a recognition that 'the quality of employees can be improved by investing in them', but this 'investment' is only in the employees as employees, to improve the quality of the work they do for the human capitalist. Arguably the term ends up dehumanizing people even more than *human resources* does, because *human capital*, like actual capital, is an immaterial and abstract measurement, merely a number on a stock-ticker. The world awaits the modern heir of Number 6 from *The Prisoner*, who will stand up and declare: 'I am not *human capital*; I am a free man!'

~

hypervising

When 'supervising' doesn't sound important enough, say you are *hypervising*. One former supervisor for Halliburton describes her duties there as 'Managing and hypervising oil field checkup.' It seems so much more dynamic. And the possible manic implications of *hyper* are kept under control by the wise scrutiny of *vising*.

In information technology, a *hypervisor* is another name for a Virtual Machine Monitor, a piece of software that creates and runs 'virtual' computers inside your computer. It's not clear whether human beings claiming that they are *hypervising* are thus trying to say that their inferiors are just mathematical constructs, or perhaps that we all really are living in the MATRIX. Whoah.

Anyway, once *hypervising* becomes a boringly common boast, there is still room for it to be extended upwards to 'ultravising'. It isn't clear whether there is an alternative in the opposite direction, 'subvising', but it could prove very useful. *Subvising* would mean what you do when you are supposed to be keeping an eye on something but can't really be bothered.

~

ideation

Have you done much *ideation* lately? You ought to. We live in an *ideation* nation. Surely only congenital thinkers-inside-the-box find the word ugly. *Forbes* calls the verb *to ideate* a 'hideous hodgepodge of "think", "plan", and "solve"', but it should go back and rant at the seventeenth century, when *ideate* began to be used to mean 'imagine' or 'conceive'. (John Donne: 'That forme of a State which Plato *Ideated*.') And *ideation* itself has been in use since the early nineteenth century, when it meant our capacity for forming ideas.

Of course modern *ideation*, like anything else, needs a specific type of management to go with it (see CHANGE MANAGEMENT). Can you guess what it's called? Yes, *ideation management*. According to one tech website: '*Ideation management*, sometimes referred to as idea management, is a formalization of the processes involved in gathering, sharing, analyzing and executing on [*sic*] ideas generated within an enterprise and its collaborative networks.' Oh, but did you see what they did there? They gave the game away by admitting that *ideation management* is sometimes called *idea management*. So *ideation* in business means nothing more than 'having ideas'.

But it certainly sounds more technical and exciting. Perhaps people hear it as a mash-up of *idea* and *creation*.

Ideation! Here is a very inspirational use of *ideation* from *Entrepreneur India* in 2013:

> Personal Branding is the art of unearthing your brand; the exclusive promise of value that Brand You offers to the world. It starts with the introspection of what makes your brand Younique, followed by the strategic *ideation* of how you will share your brand story with the world, and finally a promise – a commitment to illuminate the world with your brand, forever. I believe it is the beginning of celebrating the Brand You.

Rest assured, I am celebrating the Brand Me right now. It is totally going to illuminate the world for ever.

~

imagineering

Someone who suggests that some *imagineering* needs to be done around the office is a) extremely irritating, and b) probably not trying to make everyone think of the cheery amusements afforded by Walt Disney theme parks, even though their design is overseen by a division of the company called Walt Disney Imagineering.

Imagineer – which is just what it seems, a combination of 'imagine' and 'engineer' – is older than that, and was first used in an industrial context in the 1940s. The American company Alcoa Aluminum announced in an advert: 'For a long time we've sought a word to describe what we all work at hard here at Alcoa . . . *IMAGINEERING* is the word . . . *Imagineering* is letting your imagination soar, and then engineering it down to earth.' A bit like taking a HELICOPTER VIEW and then putting the aircraft into a DEEP DIVE? Good luck with that.

Now it is possible, of course, to engage in *imagineering leadership*, to extract even more surplus value from your workers by learning 'How to create *imagineering* employees', and even to become a Master of Imagineering by studying at the helpfully named Imagineering Academy in the Netherlands. In the summer of 2013 the magazine *Management Today* predicted, with an apparently straight face: 'It's only a matter of time before the entire staff of the

Bank of England is invited to a group *re-imagineering* of the bank's narrative.'

Personally, I have just *imagineered* a brilliant name for a new jewellery company. Imaginearring. Your ears ain't seen nothing yet.

~

impact

The UK government's website style guide counsels against
the use of *impact* as a verb, but it's a forlorn hope.
Headlines around the world in the summer of 2013
included 'Flood Claims to *Impact* General Insurers' Profit',
'Why the Haze Will *Impact* All Businesses in Singapore',
'How Will Healthcare Penalty Delays *Impact* Businesses?',
and so on. Can a delay really *impact* a business, in the sense
of physically smashing into it? I don't think so. But *impact*
sounds quite thrilling and kinetic, like a huge space rock
that is threatening to smash into earth unless Bruce Willis
can personally nuke it.

One interesting hypothesis to explain the prominence
of *to impact* (along with, shudder, the adjective *impactful*)
was offered to *Forbes* by the editor of *Black's Law Dictionary*,
Bryan Garner. He suggested that because people are
unsure of the difference between *affect* (verb) and *effect*
(noun), they avoid potential embarrassment by just using
impact interchangeably. Thus, 'We will *impact* our competi-
tor's sales with this new product', and 'Our product will
have an *impact*.' *Forbes* does slip up by calling *impact* a
'wannabe verb', since it has been used in the sense 'to
have an effect on' since at least the middle of the twentieth century. And it has been a verb since 1601 ('to pack in
tightly'), hence the dentistry term for a tooth that has not

'erupted' and is stuck below the gumline: *impacted*. To spare readers' sensibilities here, I will not also mention bowels.

Meanwhile, such is the modern sophistication of business theory that you can even analyse the way something might *impact* on your business. What's that called? *Business impact analysis*, of course. And in the world of policing and law there is such a thing as a *Community Impact Statement*, which describes the sad aftermath of a small asteroid crashing into a village.

~

inbox me

'Yeah, just *inbox* me that info.' You what? Apparently this is now an acceptable way to say 'email me' or 'send me a Facebook message' or even 'text me'. Perhaps the idea is that I am so tech-savvy and festooned with messaging accounts that I can be casually platform-neutral about it: I don't care *which* inbox it ends up in, as long as it gets there.

However, that is not a good enough excuse. If someone offers to *inbox* you, a helpful and logical reply might be to promise to *outbox* them – in other words, punch them clinically in the face until they fall down unconscious to the canvas.

~

interface

'We are moving forward to fully *interface* with our KEY STAKEHOLDERS, to really drive business outcomes in a changing environment.' So runs one actual business announcement supplied by a despairing source. Personally, when I *interface* with people, I like it to be outside the office, and I'd be nervous if they were holding stakes.

This use of the computing metaphor *to interface* – which the *New Yorker* charmingly noted in 1969 was 'a space-age verb meaning, roughly, to coordinate' – is another way in which the messy humanity of people is smoothed over by a robot-utopian vision in which everyone's parts plug into and out of everyone else's parts with a dreamy lack of friction and no uncomfortable moments the next morning.

~

issues

To call something a 'problem' is utterly verboten in the office: it's bound to a) scare the horses and b) even worse, focus responsibility on the bosses. So let us instead deploy the compassionate counselling-speak of *issues*. (This sense of 'emotional or psychological difficulties . . . points of emotional conflict' dates from the early 1980s.) The critic (and manager) Robert Potts translates 'There are some *issues* AROUND X' as 'There is a problem so big that we are scared to even talk about it directly.' Though it sounds therapeutically non-judgemental, *issues* can also be a subtly vicious way to imply personal deficiency. If you have *issues* with a certain proposal, maybe you just need to go away and work on your *issues*.

What if something is more serious than an *issue* – an incipient catastrophe that might bring down the whole business? You still can't call it a 'problem'. But you can express the very deep way in which you personally care about it by referring to it as a *concern*. How sympathetic!

~

journey

There's something peculiarly horrible about the modern bureaucratic habit of turning everything into a *journey*, with its ersatz thrill of adventurous tourism and its therapeutic implications of personal growth. Sometimes the made-up *journey* is a group affair, like a school outing. So businesses infantilize their employees by saying that they've all been on a fascinating voyage together, when in fact many of their colleagues have been brutally thrown from the bus. As one infuriated *Guardian* commenter explains, 'the "journey" we have been on' really refers to 'the ongoing cuts and redundancies in the organisation that I work for'. In other words, it's an evil journey designed by a sadistic madman so that not everyone will survive, much as in Stephen King's novel *The Long Walk*, which describes an indefinitely long walking race in which all contestants who drop below the minimum accepted speed three times are summarily killed.

Software and web designers will often talk about the *user journey*, which at least correlates with the metaphor of webpage and interface 'navigation'. But the British government also explains the process of claiming disability benefit under the rubric 'The Claimant Journey', which might be thought rather insensitive to those claimants actually unable to travel.

Enterprises who really care about how their customers

come to buy their widgets often wibble about the *customer* or *consumer decision journey*. Consulting firm McKinsey explains: 'Consumers are moving outside the purchasing funnel.' The *what*? 'Changing the way they research and buy your products.' Oh, right. 'In today's *decision journey*, consumer-driven marketing is increasingly important as customers seize control of the process and actively "pull" information helpful to them.' In other words, they, er, look up product reviews on the internet.

In Australia, people not only go on nonexistent *journeys* but also do a lot of imaginary *travelling*. 'How is the project *travelling*?', 'I'm *travelling* well', and so forth. What with all these *journeys* and jaunts being undertaken by people unmoving from their office chairs, it's a wonder the global travel industry hasn't collapsed. Of course, while it's inspiring to talk of *journeys*, managers will rarely name an exact destination or estimated time of arrival. An office *journey* can just go on and on, much like that described in the classic Talking Heads song. All together now: 'We're on a road to nowhere . . .'

~

key

With your *key* core COMPETENCIES, you wonderful thing, you can no doubt internalize the *key* LEARNINGS, ACTION the *key* DELIVERABLES, achieve the *key* performance indicators, take on *key* challenges, and overcome *key* ISSUES to meet *key* milestones and placate our *key* STAKEHOLDERS, GOING FORWARD. But why the hell is everything *key*? Is there some kind of subliminal phallic titillation to the image of *key* things PENETRATING the welcoming oiled openings of locks? Microsoft chief Steve Ballmer, for one, seems very fond of thrusting his jutting tool into relevant orifices. His hilarious 2013 'One Microsoft' memo mentions 'key innovation partners', 'key customers', 'key new technology trends', 'key partnerships', 'key developers', 'key OEM relationships', 'a key member of my leadership team', 'key technology or services', and 'key future contributors to financial success'.

Sweetly, the British government's website style guide recommends the avoidance of the adjective *key* ('A subject/thing isn't "key" – it's probably "important"'), though it has been around since the nineteenth century, and fighting it now is bootless. Even so, one does wonder whether there's anything now that can't be *key*. You can even have *key* ASKS, which are not small free-standing shops that sell newspapers or develop film. I'm tempted to start up a locksmithing business that supplies *key keys*.

Once you start calling so many things *key*, of course, semantic inflation dissolves its sense almost entirely. If everything's *key*, then nothing is any more *key* than anything else. So the incontinent spraying-around of *key* just ends up being a vague way to make everything sound grander than it really is. What is the opposite of *key*, to describe something in business that is not particularly important? I suppose it must be *hole*. Have you finished that spreadsheet yet? No, it's ON MY RADAR, but it's *hole*.

~

Kool-Aid, drink the

To *drink the Kool-Aid* means to trust blindly in what authority figures say to you, or to swallow a myth. 'Institutional investors have often swallowed the same Kool-Aid of shareholder value,' writes one brave *Forbes* contributor, mere months after the magazine crowned *drinking the Kool-Aid* the winner of its 2012 Jargon Madness competition. Starbucks CEO Howard Schultz, meanwhile, announced his disappointment with the American President in 2011 by saying that he '*drank the Kool-Aid* as much as anyone else about Obama'. (Shouldn't he have been drinking his own coffee-flavoured beverages?) Kool-Aid is an American brand of fizzy drink. So why should gulping it be such a downer?

Rather tastelessly, this phrase is a reference to the gruesome event known as the Jonestown Massacre. In Guyana in 1978, the leader of the 'People's Temple' cult, Jim Jones, had his followers drink Kool-Aid laced with cyanide, and more than 900 people died. But, contrary to the modern use of *drinking the Kool-Aid* to mean blind obedience, many members (including both adults and babies) were either forced at gunpoint to drink, or injected directly with poison. And indeed metaphorical Kool-Aid initially signified coercion: a 1982 critic of Reaganomics, for example, said that it 'administers Kool-Aid to the poor, the deprived and the unemployed'. The office would no doubt be a more interesting place if *drinking the Kool-Aid* referred to a soft drink laced with LSD, as reported in Tom Wolfe's 1968 *The Electric Kool-Aid Acid Test*, but Jonestown has drowned out those more agreeably psychedelic connotations.

Poor Kool-Aid can't be thrilled that it is now so recklessly associated with horror. (It has been claimed that the Jonestown victims drank the cheaper generic fizz Flavor Aid on that day rather than Kool-Aid, though both are visible on earlier film from the compound.) In any case, Kool-Aid's current marketing does try its best to put a happy, fun-loving face on things. 'Would you like to pour Kool-Aid at the World's Largest Kool-Aid Stand?' it asks, advertising Kool-Aid Days around America. 'Or see the smile on a small child's face when she throws a bean bag through the Kool-Aid smile?' It's just a shame they can no longer really ask: 'Would you like to see the glow in a small child's tiny eyes while she is *drinking the Kool-Aid?*' In this way, as in so many others, thoughtless office jargon hurts not only grown-up professionals but all the world's innocent children.

~

land

A high-level media executive explains to me in amazement that it is now possible to use *land* in a piloting sense for both project management and the insertion of thought-nuggets into subordinates' brains. 'Have we *landed* that project?' she explains, means 'Did we, in a spaceship-y way, manage to get it gently and safely on to the ground without crashing, and without bits falling off it?' So it's another military or astronautical metaphor. Did you *land* the project after taking a HELICOPTER VIEW while providing AIR COVER and PUSHING THE ENVELOPE?

Meanwhile, 'Have I *landed* this idea with you?' apparently means 'Have you digested and understood this idea properly?' – or, not to put too fine a point on it: 'Do you fucking get it now?' Unfortunately this use seems to be in tension with a more ordinary use of 'land': to force an unpleasant burden on someone. He's *landed* me with the bill. She's *landed* me in a heap of shit. Or maybe, after all, that's perfectly in tune with how office workers feel when they've been *landed* with what passes for an 'idea' in their boss's head.

~

learnings

Surely it is a particularly disgusting habit of the modern age to talk about the *learnings* that follow from a project or experience, rather than, say, the 'lessons'? Recently, a man at a conference literally said: 'One of the biggest *learnings* for us as an agency is the future of the intellectual property.' The word is also current in medical circles ('Twelve *Learnings* From a Transitional Care Initiative'), marketing ('*Learnings* from Mickey Mouse'), and (God help our children) education. A high-school social-studies teacher in Manila told a newspaper report on that country's education programme: 'The teachers would have to use technology and other materials for better absorption of the *learnings* by the students.'

What is wrong with all these people? Why can't they say 'lessons'? Well, perhaps in our egalitarian age 'lessons' – even in the context of school teaching – just sounds too authoritarian and strictly pedagogical. The only permissible office lessons are *lessons learned*, which are safely quarantined in the past, GOING FORWARD. Instead, *learnings* makes everyone seem as though they are on a glorious and blameless path of infinite self-improvement.

Annoyingly for those who despise the usage, however, it is not some new corporate barbarism that has sprung up recently. We know, of course, that *learning* as a singular noun is quite normal (Pope: 'A little Learning is a dang'rous Thing'). So why shouldn't you be able to pluralize it? Shakespeare, for one, saw no reason why you couldn't. In the opening scene of *Cymbeline*, the First Gentleman relates how the king adopted the orphan Posthumus and educated him: 'The king [. . .] Puts to him all the *learnings* that his time / Could make him the receiver of.' Were the groundlings grinding their teeth at this barbarous use of *learnings*? Probably not.

~

leverage

The critic Robert Potts reports this parodic-sounding but deathly real example: 'We need to *leverage* our SYNERGIES.' Other things you can *leverage*, according to recent straight-faced news and business reports, are expertise, cloud infrastructure, 'the federal data', training, and 'Hong Kong's advantages'. To *leverage*, in such examples, usually means nothing more than 'to use' or 'exploit'. Thus, '*leverage* support' means 'ask Bob in IT'; and I suggest '*leverage* the drinkables infrastructure' as a stylish new way to say 'make the coffee'.

Leverage is presumably attractive because of the imported glamour from high finance, though that might have become slightly tarnished since the global crash. But the appropriation of this financial metaphor doesn't quite seem to have been thought through. The verb *leverage* began to be used in the late 1960s specifically for a technique of 'speculating' with borrowed money. So executives who dream of *leveraging* SYNERGIES seem to be unconsciously conveying the message that they are taking a huge gamble that might result in disaster. After all, since the crash, major financial institutions around the world have been carefully *deleveraging* in order to meet new capital requirements.

The office use of *leverage*, then, hopes to borrow the

financial meaning of an enormous upside while studiously ignoring the implication of equally enormous risk. (As spread-betting companies are legally required to warn: you may lose more than your initial stake.) It is also, like so much office jargon, a way to try to *leverage* gibberish to make your actions sound more important and exciting. Unfortunately, the effect is often the opposite to that desired. Says one unhappy *Guardian* commenter: 'The use of the word "*leverage*" in my job and business in general makes me feel physically sick.'

It's also, frankly, a bit foolish-sounding. Give me a place to stand and I will move the world, said Archimedes. He didn't say he would *leverage* the DELIVERABLES MATRIX.

~

low-hanging fruit

An alpha-male executive whose testicles are so enormous that they brush the ground when he walks is often said to be possessed of *low-hanging fruit*. To *pluck the low-hanging fruit* means either to play a tune on these giant testicles, as on a lyre, or to castrate the annoying ball-dragger so that everyone else can get some peace and quiet. *We've already plucked all the low-hanging fruit* means either that the next bollock-orchestra recital is not planned till next year, or that there is no one left in the office who still owns gargantuan gonads, but there is a strange taste to the dumpling soup they've been serving in the cafeteria for days.

This modern pornographic sense of *low-hanging fruit* seems to appear only in the late 1960s, when a *Guardian* critic says of an artist that 'His rare images are picked aptly, easily, like low-hanging fruit.' It slowly became an unavoidable image in business (where some simple-minded puritans still insist it means just 'the easy stuff'). A 1988 book called *The Political Economy of Information* argues: 'Although word processing can be regarded as the leading edge of the current phase of office automation, many observers view it as simply a grab for the "*low-hanging fruit*".' That seems a peculiarly sexual attitude to word-processing, but office workers have to get their kicks where they can.

~

matrix

The *matrix* is everywhere you look in the modern office.
You can have an Accountability Matrix (aka a Responsibility
Assignment Matrix), a Functional Matrix, a Project Matrix,
a RISK Matrix, a Model Matrix and so on ad nauseam. Of
course there is even a sub-species of management called
– you guessed it – *Matrix Management*.

Are all these matrices separate universes of virtual reality
in which workers are drugged and asleep in a post-
apocalyptic world, with a virtual reconstruction of human
civilization beamed directly into their brains so the evil
masters of each *matrix* can use their bodies as batteries?

The truth is not so interesting. What is the *matrix*?
Basically, it's a spreadsheet.

~

.

mission

Personally, I only ever say that I am on a *mission* when I am a) on a five-year expedition into space, b) carrying an assault rifle as part of an elite platoon behind enemy lines, or c) roaming foreign lands dispensing Bibles. And yet the word is omnipresent in organizations of all kinds, whose workers presumably feel like Navy Seals out to 'kill or capture' a high-value target every day.

The corporate use of *mission* conveys more than just action-man glamour: following the history of the word itself, it evokes a curious blend of religious and military ideas. (A *mission* was first religious, then diplomatic, and then any kind of task, but it was not used in the modern military sense until the early twentieth century.) A company's *mission statement* is offered as a pseudo-spiritual work of philosophy, outlining not just its commercial aims (er, make as much money as possible), but also what it is pleased to call its 'values'. For instance, the *mission statement* of Starbucks literally says this: 'Our *mission*: to inspire and nurture the human spirit – one person, one cup and one neighborhood at a time.' No doubt 'one person, one cup' is a milder and more 'nurturing' version of a notoriously scatological internet video.

If a project balloons uncontrollably, it might be said to be suffering from *mission creep*. A *mission creep* is not a sweaty-faced travelling zealot who likes to grope people while telling them about God; instead the phrase is American military slang for when new objectives get added to the old ones. (This usually leads to a 'clusterfuck'.)

Meanwhile, managers around the world love to say that some things are *mission-critical*, which is an explicit invocation of shiny military hardware. (The term originated in the aerospace industry for avionics and other systems whose failure would be catastrophic.) It's true that instead of *mission-critical*, you could equally say 'essential' or 'crucial' or even just 'critical'. I mean, if something's critical it must also be *mission-critical*, right? But as with other examples of business cheerfully adding redundant words in order to bluster, preen and generally put lipstick on the pig (see SOLUTIONS), it seems that the poor language itself is suffering *mission creep*.

~

monetizing

Hey, are you *monetizing your personal brand* right now? I'm
sure I ought to be. If only I knew how. The verb *to monetize*
– meaning to turn into money – was originally applied (in
the mid-nineteenth century) to tangible things such as gold
and property. Its ubiquity today as a way of saying 'to make
money from', following the dotcom boom, seems born of
an envious desperation, as people try to *monetize* anything
they can think of, e.g. clicks or eyeballs. Note that *monetizing eyeballs* doesn't mean using eyeballs as currency, which
is just as well, since they would make your pockets all slimy.

~

moofing

It used to be the case that if you had a laptop, a Nokia, a rumpled suit, and a boarding pass, you would call yourself a *road warrior* – as though working while travelling were the equivalent of starring in *Mad Max*. Now that smartphones and ambient internet have become ubiquitous in the wondrous modern age, people can be pestered and inveigled into doing more work by colleagues no matter where they are. We need a cool new verb to describe working on the hoof, so people blackmailed into it can feel good about themselves. There already is one: *moofing*.

Moofing is what you do when you're Mobile and Out of Office. (MOOf – see what they did there?) Unfortunately for the inventor of this peculiar word, there is also a chimera or hybrid animal known as the dogcow, much loved by geeks. It was introduced as a cute pixellated icon by Apple in 1983. It even has a name – Clarus the Dogcow. And guess what sound it makes? 'Moof!'

~

move the needle

An actual human being has said: 'I thrive in situations where marketing can *move the needle*.' Perhaps we are meant to think of the needle of a seismograph, jerking in response to an earthquake, or the needle of an old-fashioned VU meter, showing the loudness of audio running through a mixing desk. Mind you, since we are talking about marketing here, it's probably more appropriate to think of the needle of a lie detector, which starts scrawling wildly when someone is speaking absolute bullshit.

When talking to venture capitalists in particular, counsels *Forbes* in its 2011 jargon contest, you should 'make clear your intentions of *moving the needle*'. What, like an incompetent acupuncturist who has to jab you again to hit the right meridian? Sadly, *Forbes* spoils such reveries by adding: 'Or you could always just say your product will be better than others.' That's not as pointy, and so much more boring.

I would only add that promising to *move the needle* is not likely to generate an enthusiastic response if you are talking to an aficionado of injectable drugs such as heroin, or an audiophile turntable enthusiast who is terrified of scratching his collection of original vinyl Rush albums. Be careful out there.

~

no-brainer

The phrase *a no-brainer* originated in sport, to describe a
physical action in football or tennis that was so well-drilled
it required no conscious thought. Its subsequent office
adoption to mean 'obviously a good idea', however, is both
inverted boast and threat. 'This is a *no-brainer*!' means not
only 'I did not engage my brain for a second in coming up
with this idea', but also 'You should not engage your brain
in any attempt to argue with it.' It is thus an announcement
and a recommendation for perfect zombie-like stupidity.

~

nurture bubble

According to my informant, a refugee from the world of advertising, one may announce the instant creation of a *nurture bubble* – ideally also miming the shape of a large bubble or egg around oneself – shortly before launching into a spiel of utter bullshit. But no one else in the meeting is allowed to complain that it is bullshit, because a *nurture bubble* exists: it is a kind of imaginary sentimental forcefield protecting the bullshitter from any challenge or criticism.

The term *nurture bubble* is used in child psychology to describe the potential danger of excessive coddling and love-smothering of children, which might do them no favours later in an indifferent or hostile world. Presumably unintentionally, the office *nurture bubble* is similarly counter-productive, since announcing it gives away the fact that you are immediately going to start talking rubbish. On the other hand, it's good for everyone else, since as long as they aren't slightly sick in their mouths when they hear the phrase *nurture bubble,* they know they can then switch off their critical faculties for the following few minutes and daydream about whatever they want, while cunningly keeping caring smiles plastered over their faces.

~

offline, take this

'Hey, can we *take this offline*?' This is a truly bizarre modern way to say 'Let's talk about it later or in private.' Oh, I'm sorry! I thought we were human beings in the same room communicating with each other by making noises with our faces! I didn't realise we were *online*. Are we all living in the MATRIX now? Is that what you mean? And if we just go down the corridor to the coffee machine and talk in pairs, we'll suddenly be *offline*? The machines didn't really think this through, did they, if that's all you have to do to escape from your prison of virtual reality? It's a wonder they managed to take over the world in the first place.

~

onboardings

Onboardings are new hires, and it is even possible to *onboard* people. So welcome on board! Our company is a giant ship – perhaps a battleship of the kind that can defeat alien spaceships (as demonstrated in the exciting film *Battleship*, surely among the best of all movies licensed from board games), or alternatively one of those cruise ships that routinely break down in the middle of the ocean, leaving passengers trapped for weeks without food or BIO-BREAK facilities and vulnerable to outbreaks of a horrible virus. Still, if no such disaster happens there's nothing to worry about except the occasional storm. (Hope you don't get seasick.)

Naturally, to keep the imagery consistent, we will henceforth describe the depressing act of firing people with the more vibrant nautical metaphor of *throwing them overboard and watching them drown.*

~

open the kimono

Guys, it's time to *open the kimono*! In creepy business
parlance, to *open the kimono* is to share information freely
with a prospective business partner or other outside party. I
don't know which is more disturbing: the possibility that
open the kimono is a sexist-Orientalist reference to ideas of
the erotically available geisha, or – perhaps even worse
– the idea that we are meant to think of a Western business-
man wearing a kimono, and opening it to reveal the glories
of his sweaty belly.

One theory has it that the phrase derives from a
Japanese expression for removing one's coat on entering a
house, and so means nothing dirtier than to relax and talk
openly. But it's still widely supposed to be snigger-worthy.
When one observer in 2010 announced that Goldman
Sachs 'needed to *open the kimono* a little bit', a rival
commentator claimed the moral high ground by decrying
this 'unfortunate expression leftover from the dot-com VC
days'. Back in those days, the *New York Times* speculated
that *open the kimono* had probably originated with 'the rash
of Japanese acquisitions of American enterprises in the
80's'. (Interested scholars will want to know, in that case,
whether Bert Cooper's use of the phrase on *Mad Men* – 'Let
them open the kimono' – was an anachronism or a schol-
arly antedating.)

In any case, it's still too tempting to abandon. In 2013 Mitch Ackles, president of the Hedge Fund Association, described the new regime of enforced reporting to government thus: 'You are going to have *to open the kimono.* There's just no way around it.' (There's just no way around the kimono. It's enormously voluminous!) The phrase can get caught up, too, in bafflingly mixed metaphors. 'If you *open the content kimono* too far,' one consultant asks, 'are you cannibalizing your ability to MONETIZE your expertise?' (Now I've been forced to visualize a cannibal snacking on the exposed flesh of a kimono-wearer. Thanks a lot.) But perhaps the most ridiculous and unintentionally insulting recent use of the phrase came in a 2012 *New York Times* profile of Mediabistro founder Laurel Touby, which enthused that her 'policy regarding her affairs is relentlessly *open kimono*'. Yep. I do appreciate you opening your kimono now and again, but could you please be a little less *relentless* about it?

~

optics

No one just *looks at* things any more, inside or outside the
office. Instead, one must consider 'how the *optics* will
resonate'. In 1704 Isaac Newton published his work *Opticks:
or, a Treatise of the Reflexions, Refractions, Inflexions and
Colours of Light.* The modern business use of *optics* trades on
the term's heritage in physics to pretend there is some kind
of reliable, scientific method to guessing what other people
will think about something. (The fact that the NSA's
communication-sucking surveillance system is called
PRISM, meanwhile, is probably a deliberately Newtonian
joke dreamed up by a waggish spy.)

Like anything else, *optics* can be managed – or at least,
people can try to do so. This amounts to deliberate decep-
tion, just as a stage illusionist manages the audience's *optics*
through clever trickery. *Forbes* writer Eric Jackson translates
'We need to manage the *optics* of this' as 'How can we lie
about this in a way people will believe?' ROBUST but
accurate.

Other metaphorical references to our peepers include
the eternal office need to pursue *clarity*, or the question of
how to *get visibility* on something. Here the idea of looking
stands in for the idea of knowing – often, sorrowfully, in a
negative sense. The gimlet-eyed Robert Potts notes percep-
tively that 'We're trying to get clarity on that' and 'We

don't have visibility on that yet' basically amount to 'We don't know and we might never know.' People also speak optically of having *focus* on something, and investigating something's *scope*, or changing it via the procedure of *rescoping*. (See also SCOPE CREEP.)

Weirdest of all in this family of images is the extremely disturbing request to *get eyes on that*. What, the recipient of such a demand might ask, are you going to pluck out your eyeballs and literally place them, gelatinous and bleeding, on the document? Or are two eyes not enough? Do you want everyone else to blind themselves ceremonially and pass the document around until it has twenty detached staring eyeballs wobbling around on its gory surface? And what are you going to do then? Line them up side-by-side and pupil-to-pupil in an eternal staring contest, and sell it as a work of conceptual art? Feed them to a sheep, in poetic revenge for all the sheep's eyeballs human beings have eaten? Have a quick game of eyeball marbles? Some people sure have a sick sense of humour.

~

pain points

Studying *pain points* is important if you wish to become a master of kung-fu fighting, sending your opponent into paroxysms of agony with a strategically placed index finger. And in business, as in the body, pain can strike anywhere. One article on 'customer relationship management' software describes the ambition to use such systems at 'all possible customer touch points', which already sounds like an unpleasant groping experience, and then mentions how the 'call agent' can discover 'the customer's *pain points*'. (Ow! Don't touch me there, it hurts!) Perhaps this is so as to stimulate them therapeutically. (Try not to MOVE THE NEEDLE.)

Alternatively, do you know how to avoid 'the five most common storage network *pain points*'? Were you aware that 'there are five primary *pain points* that banks have when it comes to understanding their mobile customers'? Yes, *pain point* is often just another creative circumlocution (see ISSUE) for the unutterable concept of a 'problem'. Confusingly, however, *pain point* is also used in marketing for an urgent customer desire or 'need' that is not yet being serviced – as though consumers are agonized junkies, desperate for an as-yet-uninvented fix. And a third sense of *pain point* describes the specific moment when people can't put up with something any more and decide to fix it once and for all: in that sense, arriving at the *pain point* is a necessary step on the path to improvement.

However *pain point* is being used, it means that something needs to change. Jeffrey Carter, a trader and 'angel investor', explains: 'Whenever I talk to entrepreneurs with business ideas, my first question to them is always, "What *pain point* are you solving?"' My first question to him is: can you really *solve* a *pain point*? To be consistent, I think the metaphor should be something like rubbing anaesthetic gel into the *pain point*, or some other traditional remedy. Personally, when I talk to entrepreneurs, I always ask them: 'What *pain point* are you trying to kiss better?'

~

paradigm shift

The term *paradigm shift* was made famous by Thomas
Kuhn's 1962 book *The Structure of Scientific Revolutions.*
There, a *paradigm* is a whole way of understanding the
world, and a *paradigm shift* is a dramatic transfiguration in
that understanding. *Paradigm shifts* are hugely important
intellectual developments such as 'the Copernican,
Newtonian, chemical, and Einsteinian revolutions'. Sadly,
owing to the widespread phenomenon of linguistic deflation, it has since become possible to call a much less
world-shattering change a *paradigm shift.* The phrase
became common during the 1990s dotcom boom as a way
for tech entrepreneurs to boost their own impressive
self-importance, though it often sounded more like wishful
thinking. (A *paradigm shift* is exactly what is needed if our
pet-focused internet start-up is actually going to make any
money.) Now in modern business-speak it's everywhere.
When gold-hoarders start selling off the metal, that's
apparently 'a *paradigm shift* in many investors' attitude
towards gold'.

One educational article in *Forbes* ambitiously begins by
sketching historic *paradigm shifts* – the Copernican revolution, Mendelian genetics, and the guy who discovered that
peptic ulcers are caused by bacteria – and then gets down
to business. Now, the author claims, 'a discontinuous

paradigm shift in management is happening. It's a shift from a firm-centric view of the world in which the firm's purpose is to make money for its shareholders to a customer-centric view of the world in which the purpose of the firm is to add value for customers.' It probably would be a *paradigm shift* (to an economic epic fail) if firms really were going to abandon all hope of making money, but that is not quite the claim here. Instead, firms are going to pretend that they are not completely self-interested and really care about their customers. In the service, of course, of making more money.

There is a British publication called *Paradigm Shift* that describes itself helpfully as 'a spiritual magazine covering lightbody activation, spiritual enlightenment, reiki, spiritual healing, and kundalini'. This perhaps represents a *paradigm shift* from trying to understand the world rationally to taking a DEEP DIVE into the world of woo-woo and never again coming up for air. Yet even this use might after all be closely related to the overuse of *paradigm shift* in office-speak. After all, to say 'This is a *paradigm shift*!' is a very useful way of sounding technical and intellectually superior while quietly admitting that you have no idea why the company is suddenly haemorrhaging money.

~

penetration

Market penetration: sex behind a fruit stall. *Penetration pricing*: a courtesan's tariff. *Android penetration*: sex with robots.

~

person specification

It's familiar to anyone who has filled out a job application in modern times, but to my mind *person specification* – the bit of the job ad that describes the required qualifications and other COMPETENCIES – is a particularly brutalizing piece of modern HR jargon. *Specification* more usually means the technical details of a computer or other piece of machinery, so *person specification* brings to mind the image of creating a human being from the ground up by choosing various off-the-shelf components, until one has created the perfectly customized slave. In this way the employer becomes a kind of creator demi-god, supernaturally able to *specify* a particular *person*, just as in the real world one can specify a cutting-edge PC to run the latest grenade-festooned video game. Oh, do I not meet your *person specification*? That's too bad. Maybe you can grow the right person in a vat.

~

prepone

This is the opposite of 'postpone', so logically *prepone* should mean to do something before now. How this is possible without access to a time machine is one of the great mysteries of the modern workplace.

Well, all right, there is another possibility: since postponing means moving to a later date, *preponing* could mean bringing forward to an earlier date, but still one in the future. Although this might sound like a glib twenty-first-century coinage by feckless corporate word-poisoners, the word is actually a cool century old. Helpfully, it was coined explicitly by a writer in the *New York Times*, J.J.D. Trenon: 'For the benefit mainly of the legal profession in this age of hurry and bustle,' he wrote, 'may I be permitted to coin the word "*prepone*" as a needed rival of that much revered and oft-invoked standby, "postpone".' Why yes, Mr Trenon, you may.

The word subsequently became popular in Indian and South Asian political and business English during the 1980s and 1990s, and is now creeping into the rest of the Anglosphere – though if this implies that everyone these days is keener than ever to get their work done before the original deadline, I never got that memo.

~

proactive

People have long hated *proactive*. It seems an unnecessary jargonizing of 'active'. When Isaac Newton was writing down his laws of physics, he did not feel the need to say: 'To every proaction there is an equal and opposite reaction.'

Nonetheless, these days 'active' simply would not sound 'pro' enough. In business parlance, *proactive* seems to have been adopted (starting in the 1960s) because of the balancing symmetry it provides with the name of a quality that is now widely understood to be a mortal commercial sin – that is, being *reactive*. How appalling to be reactive; how splendid to be *proactive*.

The bible of the project-management methodology PRINCE2 lists among its own 'benefits' that of 'Being *proactive*, not reactive, but also able to accommodate sudden, unexpected events.' Um, hang on. If you can 'accommodate' unexpected events, surely that means you are able to *react* to them appropriately? So you must be '*proactive*, not reactive', but also, er . . . reactive? So confusing.

It turns out that there is a good reason for the word *proactive* in a completely different context: the psychology of learning and memory. Here 'proactive' is not the opposite of 'reactive' but of 'retroactive'. What is *retroactive* works on something in the past; what is *proactive* works on something in the future. As a 1933 psychology text defines them, a 'retroactive inhibition' suppresses learning that has already been accomplished; while a '*proactive* inhibition' will suppress future learning. So it turns out that the original sense of *proactive* is pleasingly relevant to modern work-life after all: too much office jargon is very likely to act as a *proactive inhibition* on the future LEARNINGS of its defenceless victims.

I suspect that when a manager tells subordinates he wants them to be *proactive*, what he really means is: 'I want you to read my mind and save me the bother of telling you what to do, even though that is actually my job.' Clever.

~

productize

OMG, really? Yep, *productize* is now a verb. Guess what it means? That's right – to turn something into a product. It's a bit like MONETIZE, only less brashly confident of actually making money. (Maybe no one will buy the product, but at least it will exist.) Things that are *productized* are often surprisingly abstract. A friend reports that he once heard in a tech-company meeting the phrase 'create a value proposition around *productizing* soft objects'. What, selling pillows and guinea pigs? Sadly, 'soft objects' are just any abstract or intangible things, such as software, design and so forth.

Another soft object, presumably, is knowledge. Did you know that you can also *productize* that? Sure, says Investopedia: 'For example, a person can *productize* their expertise by putting it into a tangible object by creating a product based on that knowledge.' Wait, I think I'm doing that right now! Please shoot me.

~

punch a puppy

What kind of sadist would *punch a puppy*? Ah, that is exactly the point. According to *Forbes*, to *punch a puppy* means to do something detestable – to perform an action that will attract odium, even though it's necessary for the business.

Curiously, the same idea used to be expressed by the more trigger-happy expression *shoot the puppy*. According to Tony Thorne's book of that title on 'the curious jargon of modern life', this phrase originated in a satirical fantasy by a 1980s television producer, who speculated that some people might volunteer to shoot a puppy on television just to get their fifteen minutes of fame.

In some ways, *punching* a puppy sounds more up-to-date, in a muscular and Ultimate Fighting Championship way, than shooting it, and arguably less cowardly. Without a gun, after all, it's a fair fight between you and the puppy. Or perhaps it's just that by now, fearless business leaders have shot so many puppies that they have simply run out of bullets, and are reduced to punching the baby dogs in their adorable furry faces.

~

push the envelope

Whenever I hear the phrase *push the envelope* I cannot help picturing a dejected postman shuffling along the street in a squatting position, shoving a filthy item of mail along the rough ground with outstretched fingers. Granted, that seems a pretty inefficient method of mail delivery. In fact, to *push the envelope* – meaning to attempt the previously untried – is another importation of military slang into the sedate world of office politics.

The aeronautical term 'flight envelope' means the boundary of normal operating limits (altitude, speed, and so forth) of the aircraft. Thus, to *push the envelope* is to make the craft operate outside normal parameters. This term became current among NASA test pilots during the 1970s, and a variant was popularized by Thomas Wolfe's astronaut-fancying tome *The Right Stuff*: 'One of the phrases that kept running through the conversation was "pushing the outside of the envelope" . . . [That] seemed to be the great challenge and satisfaction of flight test.'

Perhaps next time this phrase comes up in a meeting, someone could point out mildly that *pushing the envelope* can – and in under-qualified hands almost certainly will – result in a fatal malfunction that leads to the irretrievable loss of craft and crew.

~

quality

The ubiquitous business use of *quality* has become a kind of totem. Now it has been cut loose from having to be the quality *of* anything in particular, we can all sit around happily chanting that *quality* is our aim – or, in other words, that we want stuff to be . . . er, good? The hopeful invocation of *quality* is magical speech that hopes to conjure into being something that is indefinable but definitely better than flat-out rubbishness.

But the insertion of *quality* into a business slogan or MISSION statement is also sometimes camouflage for less sunny intentions. In Britain, the National Health Service has a governing wheeze known as 'Quality, Innovation, Productivity and Prevention', or QIPP for short. My NHS informant darkly alleges that – as one might infer from the concentration on 'savings' in the QIPP literature – 'It's basically about firing people.' Meanwhile, in 2011, the BBC grandly announced that its plan over the next six years would be called 'Delivering Quality First'. (Rather than delivering TV and radio programmes first? Or perhaps they meant delivering quality first and garbage later?) But this slogan was merely a cravenly euphemistic sticking-plaster for a programme of mass redundancies. Delivering Quality First actually meant sacking 2,000 workers.

Of course, if you want your business's *quality* to be even

more, um, *quality*, you can take up Total Quality Management (rather than Half-Arsed Quality Management or Total It-Will-Do Management), and institute work milestones known as Quality Gates (hey, that *is* a quality gate, what with all the nicely worked wrought iron). You can also select a group of lucky employees to form a Quality Circle. This does not mean getting them to stand in a formation of perfect roundness, but just asking them to talk to one another now and again to see whether things could be improved. I suggest incentivizing the hapless employees so suborned into a Quality Circle by giving them a tin of Quality Street.

Quality comes from the Latin word *qualitas* ('distinguishing characteristic, essential character or nature'), which was invented by Cicero as an equivalent for the Greek *poiotes*. That is first found in Plato's dialogue *Theaetetus*, where Socrates apologizes for using it, calling it a 'strange word'. Not much has changed in two and a half millennia. When Honda says that *quality* is a 'core value', what is that supposed to mean except 'We try not to make shit cars'?

~

radar, on my

'It's *on my radar.*' Wow, you have *radar*! That's so cool. Is it
wired directly into your brain so that everywhere you look
there is a little radar screen in the corner of your vision with
green and red blobs moving on it, as in a first-person shooter
videogame? Or do you have a little gizmo in your pocket that
you slap out at opportune moments and which shows you
people, objects, and immaterial slices of makework in a
glowing green representation of three-dimensional space?
Or are you just pleased to see me?

The office use of *radar* is obviously a macho military
borrowing, but it also has a more wily function. The handy
thing about radar is that it tells you not only that enemy
aircraft are present and in which direction, but how far
away they are. (Hence the US Navy's derivation of the word
from the phrase 'RAdio Detection And Ranging'.) So to say
that something is *on my radar* can be a subtle way of
announcing that, since it's not close enough right now to
be worth bothering myself with, I'm planning to do exactly
sod all about it, so will you please go away now?

~

reach out

Someone might not want to TOUCH (your) BASE, but they could still threaten to *reach out*. 'I just wanted to *reach out* and . . .' What? Touch me? This is not a Depeche Mode song. Keep your filthy paws to yourself. I suppose that with everyone *reaching out* all the time, some of them must be reaching out while CIRCLING BACK, which technically counts as a reacharound.

This kind of metaphorical *reaching out* (for variety's sake, you can also call it 'outreach') used to denote explicitly an offer of support or assistance, when it first came into use a century ago (the US government wanted to *reach out* to low-income families, et cetera). The office use of *reach out*, however, implies more of a pestilent grasping. It also reminds me of the nightmares I used to have about Mr Tickle, from Roger Hargreaves's *Mr Men* series of children's books. Mr Tickle is a round, smiling orange man with a blue bowler hat and amazingly long, stretchy arms. He can *reach out* through several rooms or across the street to tickle you when you are least expecting it, in the middle of the night. These days he would probably be arrested.

~

reports

Reports are usually pointless documents: as the book of
Ecclesiastes was already lamenting millennia ago, 'Of the
making of *reports* there is no end, and much LEARNINGS is a
weariness to the flesh.' But now *reports* can also be people
– as in the genuine instruction one amazed worker offers:
'CASCADE THIS DOWN to your direct *reports*'. (In other words,
those who 'report' directly to you.) And Steve Ballmer's
inspirational 'One Microsoft' memo of July 2013 enthused:
'Each major initiative will have a champion who will be a
direct *report* to me or one of my direct *reports*.'

This usage certainly sounds less hierarchical than
underlings or *subordinates*, but also less pseudo-egalitarian
than TEAM. It's also another small way in which the humanity of workers is denied: calling them *reports* pictures them
as nothing more than paper cut-outs. I suppose that's
better, at least, than intending the sense of *report* as the
noise made when a gun goes off, which would characterise
your inferiors merely as a series of loud bangs.

~

repurposing

Repurposing just means recycling, but it sure sounds more purposeful. Business tools and systems can be *repurposed*, which just means 'used in a new way'. So – more alarmingly – can people, as though they were reprogrammable automata into whose heads we just need to upload a new instruction set. (In some sad cases, a *repurposing* might really be a TRANSITIONING, i.e. a sacking: the notional android now destined to wander the desolate wastes and end up as battery-drained landfill.)

After you have finished it, you may decide to *repurpose* this book as a handy platform for the construction of jazz cigarettes, or as a doorstop. Good luck!

~

resizing

Once upon a time, companies that sacked people were said to be *downsizing*. But that came to sound too negative – a bit of a downer – and so it gradually gave way to *rightsizing*. Perhaps because *rightsizing*, on the other hand, has a ring of hubris that might become a hostage to fortune ('We know exactly the right size for our company!'), it is now being challenged by the apparently more modest *resizing*.

Resizing does have an amusingly neutral sartorial tone, as though you are sending your trousers to the tailors to adjust the waistline. But companies never *resize* upwards. Instead they will start boasting about 'job creation'. (It is notable that when they are sacking people, on the other hand, they never announce a vast programme of 'job destruction'.)

The point of all these euphemisms for sacking people (DEMISING, 'cost leadership', 'rationalization', 'managing out') is twofold: first, it insulates the boss class from the emotional violence of what they are doing – taking people's livelihoods away from them. Second, it reassures the employees who are left that someone upstairs actually has a clue what they are doing. As management professor Jennifer Chatman told CNN: 'Companies have to reassure the people who are left that there's a plan in place. People see through what executives say, but what unnerves people the most is believing that nobody has control over anything.'

Logically, the next stage on the euphemism treadmill after *downsizing, rightsizing* and *resizing* ought to be *funsizing*. A just-fired worker will be able to confide gigglingly down the pub that he has been 'funsized', and the whole sad business of sacking people will be imbued with an irresistibly playful tone.

~

revert

'Let me *revert* . . .' is a common way now of promising to do
something that already had a lot of perfectly good and
simple words to describe it. Reply? Respond? Whatever was
wrong with those? (To be fair, *revert* could mean 'to return to
a person' in medieval times, so it's not a wholly novel usage.)
While *revert* is less infuriatingly circuitous than CIRCLE BACK,
there is still something sonically rather unlovely about it.
(Perhaps it is the echo of 'pervert'.) I do recommend that if
anyone ever promises to *revert back* to you, you should shout
as loudly as you can that this means 'get back back', and
then start doing a bad chimp dance with optional hooting
noises. Alternatively, since the verb *revert* originally meant 'to
regain consciousness', you can reply to a promise to *revert* by
wishing the offender sweet dreams.

~

rightshoring

When they give your job to a Chinese worker for a tenth
of the pay, your job has been *rightshored*. In contrast to the
older term *outsourced*, which keeps attention focused on
the sad movement away from here, *rightshoring* reassures
us all that the job is now in the correct geographical
location, the country it was always supposed to live in, as
though it were a generously repatriated refugee. If
rightshoring isn't convincing enough to your sceptical
workforce, you can go one better by announcing a
programme of *bestshoring*. Then surely no one will dare
disagree that management knows best.

~

ringfence

A *ringfence* is a fence made entirely of rings – wedding rings, signet rings, owl rings, and so forth. It is thus very expensive but very sturdy, and just the right thing for metaphorically insulating one operation or department or pile of money in your business from another.

In politics, where the term is endemic, you can *ringfence* a single thing (e.g. health spending), which just means to protect it. (This comes from the more boring alternative sense of *ringfence* that means, um, a fence that goes all the way around something.) More weirdly, though, it is rhetorically possible to *ringfence* one thing from another, e.g. the retail and investment operations of banks. Of course in the latter case the closed circle of a *ringfence* no longer really makes metaphorical sense. (Are we talking one ring or two?) You might as well just say *fence off*.

But who ever heard of politicians simplifying language? Instead, announcing new banking rules in early 2013, the sneering faux-prole-accented British chancellor, George Osborne, happily declared: 'In the jargon, we will *electrify the ringfence*.' He thus broke the government's own style guide, which counsels against any use of *ringfence*. But the poor chap probably couldn't help it, dreaming evilly as he no doubt was of the smell of crisping human flesh from countless innocents electrocuted by his fatal partition.

~

risk

Spreadsheet-jockeying is a perilous affair. Intrepid managers brave all kinds of hazards, the likes of which would
make John Rambo curl up in a foetal position and start
crying. There are *risks* everywhere one looks. This little
word is a handy way to enhance one's own image of
daredevil heroism while avoiding, as usual, the utterly
forbidden word 'problem' (even in the context of merely
potential problems). A real-life company memo, for
instance, promises soporifically: 'There will also be a
cross-departmental steering group set up, which will work
from next week to drive the project through, identify *risks*
and plan for their management and mitigation.'

Ah yes, their *management*. There is nothing on this Earth
or only in people's heads that cannot be managed once a
business-theory programme to do so has been dreamed up.
The science of *risk management*, in particular, is a magical
way of pretending you know how to avoid future disaster.
(The reliability of this science was most effectively demonstrated by the global financial meltdown of 2008.) In fact,
what *risk management* really means to its promoters, explains
analyst Emma Sheldrick, is 'getting an exit plan in place so
when things go wrong there are some ready-made excuses
at hand'.

~

robust

Ah, *robust*. A splendidly flexible adjective that is used in so many contexts that it often turns out to mean simply 'not completely terrible'. So, for example, a desire to have *robust systems* in place expresses the impossible dream that Microsoft Office won't crash every hour.

Speaking of Microsoft Office, the business use of *robust* probably comes from statistical analysis via software engineering. In statistics, a test that is *robust* will give the correct result even if some of the inputs change or are wrong. So a computer program that is *robust* can recover from errors rather than simply crashing. If we pursue the analogy into the corporate world, we can see that a CEO's position is *robust* if he drives the company into near-bankruptcy but still receives a $100 million payoff.

In a darker mood, a long-established use of *robust* in English is to mean, euphemistically, 'unfancy', or even positively rude ('*robust* manners') or crude ('*robust* thinking'). And so it is with *robust management*, which one *Guardian* commenter straightforwardly translates as 'acting like a total cunt'.

Robust, therefore, can be a nasty little way of rhetorically disguising viciousness as healthy strength. Say what you like about Adolf Hitler, but his *Mein Kampf* was surely a powerful example of *robust* THOUGHT LEADERSHIP.

~

scope creep

When a project's remit snowballs. Also: a voyeur with a
sniper rifle.

~

sense check

A *sense check* is when you go through your senses one by one
and check that they are all functioning normally. Vision?
Check. Smell? Check. And so on. Alternatively, a *sense check*
is what a punctilious restaurant critic performs, verifying
not only the taste but the touch and the sound of the food.

In the office, though, a *sense check* is not so sensuous a
procedure. The University of Bedfordshire's business
'knowledge hub' offers advice on how to present a bid for a
tender: 'You may have written ten paragraphs of great
prose but take the time to *sense-check* that you have actually
answered the question, concisely and clearly.' Here,
sense-check just means, er, check. Paradoxically, the extra
'sense' adds no sense at all.

Or perhaps you want to do a *sense check* of your marketing plan? This means checking that it is not a face-meltingly
stupid plan. A *sense check* reassures the checker that what is
being checked is not utter nonsense. Apparently this has to
be done so often that it now has a special name, which does
not imply flattering things about business logic in general.

~

silos

Everyone in business hates wheat-storage SOLUTIONS, or so
you'd imagine from the constant calls to *tear down the silos*
and free ourselves from the *silo mentality*. Or perhaps,
unusually for office jargon, there is some kind of subliminal anti-war message implied: after all, nuclear missiles are
stored in *silos*, and bombs designed to break through their
concrete bunkers are sometimes called *silo-busters*.
Presumably military commanders who want their subordinates to talk to one another don't ever use the metaphor of
breaking down the silos, since some eager recruit might
misunderstand and blow the bloody doors off.

~

singing from the same hymnsheet

The wish to have everyone *singing from the same hymnsheet* is a weird, happy-clappily religious metaphor to use in the office, but it's also fundamentally stupid. I mean, have you ever watched a choir in a church? They are not all *singing from the same hymnsheet*. They have one each. Otherwise they'd have to huddle round in a tight little circle, craning their necks to share a single sorry piece of manuscript paper. That would plainly result in ergonomic and musical disaster.

~

solutioning

Solutioning – to mean 'finding a solution' – is one of those words ordinary workers hate so much that they sometimes say: 'It's not a real word.' Unfortunately, it is now. Indeed, it has been for quite a while in a different context: since the late nineteenth century, *solutioning* has meant the process of applying a (chemical) solution to something, either to treat it or to stick it to something else. *Solutioning* in this old sense features in many twentieth-century texts about geology, dam-building, and nuclear energy.

The modern sense of *solutioning* that means 'finding solutions' – i.e. what in a simpler age was called *solving* – first appears in the 1990s in the context of therapy and counselling. Thus its importation into business-speak is parallel with that of ISSUES to describe problems, and probably for the same reason. After all, if you say 'problem-solving' you are acknowledging the existence of problems, which in business must never be done. So *solutioning* becomes a handy circumlocution.

These days we can enjoy *creative solutioning* or *solutioning unconventionally*, and anything that was once called a 'service' or a 'product' sounds so much more helpful (as well as usefully vague on the details) if you instead rebrand it as a *solution*. IT firms offer *enterprise solutions*, and one bank offers what it calls *lending solutions*, which I'm pretty sure just means 'loans'. Silicon Valley start-up Blackjet offers 'the most affordable private jet charter *solution*', though that might be rather a niche market. A friend even reports that he has seen a door company that offers, in a phrase superbly resistant to parody, *exit solutions*.

A good way to check whether *solutions* are corporate bullshit is just to see whether anything is lost when you remove the word *solutions*. For instance, the storage company Access says on its buildings that it offers 'storage *solutions*'. In other words: storage.

The positive-at-all-costs tone of *solutioning* and *solutions* also provides us with another inventive euphemism for the banned word 'problem'. As the astronaut Jack Swigert famously said during the near-catastrophic Apollo 13 mission: 'Houston, we have a *solution opportunity*.'

~

soup to nuts, from

From soup to nuts – meaning 'from start to finish', as in some
weird meal that begins with soup and ends with nuts – must
confuse peoples with more civilized eating habits than the
English in some soft-porn 1970s home-catering guide. The
equivalent Roman expression was *from egg to apples*, which
sounds curiously healthy. But who the hell serves nuts last?
Apparently it used to be the thing to do in America, from
where the phrase originates in the early twentieth century.
(Laurel and Hardy play butlers in a 1928 short film called
From Soup to Nuts.) And nuts were (and perhaps still are in
some rarefied places) served with port at the end of a
formal meal. (See W.H. Auden's 1947 *New Yorker* review of
T.S. Eliot's *Notes Towards a Definition of Culture*, entitled
'Port and Nuts with the Eliots'.) I don't remember seeing
any nuts in my port-quaffing days, but then I was very, very
drunk at the time.

~

spiders, we're not here to fuck

'Shall we start the meeting?'

'We're not here to fuck spiders.'

'Can I finalize that document?'

'We're not here to fuck spiders.'

'Do you want a coffee?'

'We're not here to fuck spiders.'

This isn't really an office-specific phrase – I was introduced to it by an Australian friend as a vividly affirmative way to reply to the offer of another drink in a bar. ('Shall I get more beers?' 'We're not here to fuck spiders.') But I think the work-day could be brightened immeasurably if everyone used it as often as possible. *We're not here to fuck spiders.*

~

stakeholders

Stakeholders are people in the company who are affected by a certain project; also, sometimes, business partners and customers. This term, plump with cheaply bought respect, seems to have infected corporate-speak from its ubiquity in New Labour politics, where *stakeholders* were not wooden-spike-wielding vampire hunters but people with an interest (usually financial) in some issue.

Curiously, this was itself a complete reversal of meaning: from 1708, a *stakeholder* was originally the disinterested party who *held* the *stakes* on behalf of others who were making a wager. The *stakeholder* thus had no skin in the game at all. But the inverted political sense is of surprisingly early origin too: a *Times* editorial of 1821 could already speak of 'all good subjects of the same Government' being '*stakeholders* in one system of liberty, property, laws, morals, and national prosperity'.

Manager and analyst Emma Sheldrick offers some useful translations of its modern office usages. *Manage our stakeholders*, she explains, means 'Placate the people who are asking the intelligent questions about why something is being done'; while *Update our stakeholder* MATRIX really signifies: 'We need to take off the people who disagree with the task at hand and find some new ones who agree.' If someone is being difficult or just not showering your embryonic project with sufficient appreciation, you can simply decide that, actually, they're not a real *stakeholder* after all. Call them *stakedroppers* and ruthlessly wipe them from your mind.

~

strategy

Every executive is a little Napoleon, and no business
ambition is complete without a grandiose reference to
strategy, which is some plan or at least hope that is meant to
last further than the weekend.

The origin of *strategy* is military (it comes from the Greek
for the command of a general), but it has long been used
in other fields: in the nineteenth century, one could
already speak of political strategy, or the strategy of a
philosophical argument. The business use, however, seems
to arise no earlier than the 1960s, probably inspired by the
talk of *strategy* in the new field of game theory during the
previous decade. Now, of course, *strategy* is infecting even
traditionally sedate institutions such as universities, where
its deployment is a KEY indicator of widespread despair
among dons. In early 2013 one newly appointed Pro-Vice-
Chancellor perpetrated the extraordinary sentence: 'This is
a very exciting time to join Liverpool John Moores
University as it has a clear *strategic* vision focused on
LEVERAGING mutually beneficial relationships with business,
government and the arts to strengthen its position as one
of Liverpool's nationally significant and internationally
renowned institutions.' And there was I thinking a university was for teaching and research.

Strategy is usually contrasted with tactics. (An 1818

military dictionary puts it this way: '*Strategy* differs materially from *tactic*; the latter belonging only to the mechanical movement of bodies, set in motion by the former.') In reality, business *strategy* is often just a tactic; but with a more long-term plan – or perhaps *overarching strategy* – the detailed tactics will be called the *strategy* 'execution' or 'implementation'. It is even possible, according to the management literature, to have a *strategy execution plan*, in other words a plan to execute your plan, or a *strategy* about fulfilling your *strategy*. Probably you can then have a *strategy* about the precise *strategy* to follow in order to implement your *strategy* – a *strategy execution plan scheme* – and so on. It's strategies all the way down.

The despised verbing *to strategize* was already in use in American political circles during the 1940s, but is now the preferred activity of high-level BLUE-SKY thinkers in corporations around the world. No doubt they happily bed-hop with *strategic partners*, managing the chronological logistics of this with the help of a *strategic agenda*, and are also blessed with *strategic agility*, which is an impressive ability to replace your idiotic *strategy* with another one at a moment's notice.

~

sunset

This is an imagistic verbing – 'We're going to *sunset* that project/service/version' – that sounds more humane and poetic than 'cancel' or 'kill' or 'stop supporting'. When faced with the choice between calling a spade a spade and cloying euphemism, you know which the bosses will choose. (Happily, *sunsetting* also sounds less smelly than the venerable old *mothballing*.) One stout *Guardian* defender of jargon complains that there is nothing wrong with *sunsetting* because 'It typically refers to something that is being retired because it has come to the end of its natural life. Which is not the same as being "cancelled" or "killed".'

I don't know about you, but if someone told me I was *being retired* because I had come to *the end of my natural life*, I would be quite alarmed that this itself was a euphemism for murdering me.

~

synergy

In *7 Habits of Highly Successful People*, Stephen Covey's
blockbusting 1989 self-help tome, habit number six is
synergizing. 'To put it simply,' Covey writes, '*synergy* means
two heads are better than one.' Surely that depends? I
mean, two heads work well for Zaphod Beeblebrox in
Hitchhiker's Guide to the Galaxy, but then he is an alien.

Marketers love to exploit (or LEVERAGE) synergies, and
corporations boast of the *synergy* promised by a merger.
Synergy being such an unquestioned virtue, it is also a
popular term in company names. These days you can quaff
Synergy drinks and wear Synergy organic clothing while
working out at a Synergy fitness club. Then you can travel
to Greece for some Synergy plastic surgery.

Such a trip would be quite appropriate, for the word
synergy was built from the Greek for 'working together'. In
the nineteenth century it was used to describe how the
organs of the human body function in harmony, and then
in the 1950s it was applied to the psychology of group
behaviour when humans cooperated with one another.
Consciously or not, this use represented a revival of the
meaning of *synergy* from its earliest recorded use, in 1660,
when a writer speaks of 'a Synergie, or cooperation, as
makes men differ from a sensless stock, or liveless statua'.

It's not then much of a step to borrow *synergy* for

business-speak, and indeed it crops up in a 1965 book entitled *Corporate Strategy*. 'We begin to explore *synergy*,' the author, H.I. Ansoff, writes exploratorily. 'It is frequently described as the "2 + 2 = 5" effect to denote the fact that the firm seeks a product–market posture with a combined performance that is greater than the sum of its parts.' (It's tickling to see this early use of a firm seeking a 'posture', as though there were a mass yoga demonstration in the office every day.)

So this is what *synergy* has now come to mean: the promise that the whole can be greater (by which is usually meant more profitable) than its separate parts, given the magic fairy dust sprinkled by executives busily *synergizing* all day. Perhaps it makes you sad that the term's original celebration of human cooperation has been carefully depersonalized. But this is probably just as well, since the *synergy* promised by corporate mergers usually results in humans being summarily ejected from the synergistically RESIZED mothership.

Announcements of *synergy* in the modern office, of course, are more usually hope than accurate prediction. This would not surprise the scientist and inventor Buckminster Fuller, who invented the geodesic dome and has a carbon molecule (buckminsterfullerene) named after him. According to Fuller, *synergy* in the context of systems theory meant that the behaviour of the whole could *not* be predicted from knowledge of the behaviour of the parts. So in that sense, business *synergy*, like so much else, is really an unknowable gamble.

~

takeaway

A *takeaway* in British English is what Americans call a takeout: food, often of an ersatz Chinese or Indian style, to be consumed off the premises where it is purchased. It is now used in the office to mean the information you should retain after a meeting: the greasy, unhealthy thought-noodles whose sauce will leak into the bottom of the brown paper bag while you are striding away in relief, possibly causing the base of the bag to disintegrate and your *takeaway* to spill all over the floor.

Of course, if a meeting has only a singular *takeaway* (rather than, say, multiple LEARNINGS), it follows that most of the meeting was a complete waste of time, and it could profitably have been compressed into the time it takes simply to recite the *takeaway*. (Efficiency fetishists might even suggest that, in this case, the *takeaway* could just be sent to everyone as an email, thus saving the time, distraction and possible offensive odours of holding a meeting in the first place.)

Perhaps in order to head off this alarming conclusion, the word KEY is sometimes added in order – as it always does – to make the term sound more important. A *key takeaway* is first among *takeaways*. If you take away nothing else, take away the *key takeaway*. Were there other *takeaways*? You can't remember any more, because you didn't take them away. Can we stop taking things away now?

~

team

Ah, the *team*. Are you a *team player*? (Anecdotal responses to
'There's no I in *team*' include 'No, but there are five in
individual brilliance', and the rather more forthright 'No,
but there is a U in cunt.') Have you been on a *team-building
exercise*? Are you *on the team*? ('I'm not *on* the *team*,'
complains one sufferer, 'I'm *in* the fucking *team*!') The
workplace is apparently a delightful arena of eternal play
among a Premiership of *teams* all happily working together
for the good of their comrades. How equitable. It's almost
as though no one is being exploited for profit.

In fact the sporting metaphor of the *team* is, as Melissa
Gregg notes in her excellent book *Work's Intimacy*, one of
the most subtly coercive aspects of modern office life.
'The *team* is the mythically egalitarian playing field in
which all colleagues work together, sharing responsibility
for the organization,' she writes. Workers who are thus
persuaded by management rhetoric that they are in a *team*
are – handily for management – ready to do extra work so
as not to let down their fellow *team*-members: 'Loyalty to
the *team* has the effect of making extra work seem courte-
ous and common sense, which is particularly problematic
for poorly compensated part-time workers.' Meanwhile,
Gregg says, 'teamwork rhetoric' also helps to excuse
'inadequate staffing levels'. The office *team*, then, is a kind

of enforced hallucination of communist mutual aid that distracts attention from the continuing realities of hierarchy and power.

If it's bad enough being 'on' a *team*, imagine being on a *tiger team*. A *tiger team*, *Forbes* explains, is 'a bunch of tech geeks entrusted with curing your computer ills'. This is a particularly strange metaphor since tigers are splendidly solitary predators, and no one has ever seen a *team* of tigers in the wild working together to discombobulate an antelope.

~

thinking outside the box

Here is a big cardboard box. It's big enough to crawl into, curl up small, and close the lid, inhaling that nice cardboardy smell and enjoying the protective gloom. But on no account should you do any thinking in it. The box is rigged with sensors tuned to detect telltale electrical signals of rational activity. If they do, they will set off a small but fatal explosion. The next time someone opens the box they will see that you are dead. So if you need to do any thinking, remember to do it only outside the box.

Quantum physicists will recognize this as a version of Schrödinger's cat paradox, which isn't the origin of *thinking outside the box* either. In fact it derives from the slang sense of 'box' to mean 'vagina'. It was famously said of a debauched minor lord and notorious cocksman in the early seventeenth century that, if he wanted to avoid squandering his fortune entirely, he would have to learn to think outside the box as well as in it.

I'm afraid I just made that up, because the truth is more mundane. There exists a puzzle in which you have to try to connect nine dots arranged in a square grid on a piece of paper by drawing four straight lines in one continuous motion. You can only do this, remarks a 1970 *OED* citation, if you 'think outside the dots': the lines must extend beyond the 'box' of dots. Alternatively, a 1971 book on data management explained the phrase this way: 'If you have kept your thinking process operating inside the lines and boxes [of organization charts], then you are normal and average, for that is the way your thinking has been programmed.'

Through a kind of deflation by overuse, by now *thinking outside the box* just means coming up with an idea that isn't the most obvious and shatteringly stupid one possible. It is such a cliché that anyone who uses the phrase *think outside the box* is incapable of, er, thinking outside the box. But it still has that viciously patronizing feel, assuming that anyone you address it to is trapped in a little mental prison of cowardly conformity, and only an exceptional leader such as yourself can help free them by using such inspirational language as, er, *think outside the box.*

Meanwhile, if you are ever assigned, as was one unfortunate *Guardian* commenter, to a *box* TEAM – a TEAM charged with, yes, *thinking outside the box* – you might as well pack in your job altogether. Think of all the lovely, real corrugated-cardboard boxes you could use to carry away a) your personal belongings and b) a lifetime's worth of free stationery, before they relieve you of your swipecard.

~

thought leader

A *thought leader* is someone who deposits a steaming package of pure thought in his wake and then runs away to a safe distance before it explodes, utterly destroying everything within an impressive blast radius.

Or maybe a *thought leader* is akin to a squadron leader, fronting an aerial formation of pure thought, directing a pack of offensive flying machines that are nothing more than potent mental constructs firing missiles of WEAPONIZED notions.

Alternatively, a *thought leader* is someone who drags thought in unheard-of new directions, striking out like a fearless conceptual pioneer into the vast interstellar space of the previously unthought. A thought leader thinks the unthinkable. Except of course you can't actually think the unthinkable. Because it's unthinkable.

Those to whose delicate ears *thought leader* sounds like offensively clumsy modern jargon might be disappointed to learn that the term was already being used back in the nineteenth century. One writer in 1872 praised the essayist and poet Ralph Waldo Emerson for manifesting 'the wizard power of a *thought-leader*'. Approving references to *thought leaders* also appeared periodically in Unitarian writings by people who exhorted the power of free thinking – which seems a bit paradoxical. Why would 'free thinkers', of all people, want a leader to tell them what to think?

~

thought shower

The term 'brainstorm' is now discouraged, since some people think it's insensitive to people with epilepsy, on the dubious basis that an epileptic attack is like a storm in the brain. In fact, the National Society for Epilepsy surveyed its members in 2005 as to whether they found the term 'brainstorming' offensive, and a large majority said no. Nevertheless, it is more common these days to be invited to a *thought shower*, which no doubt sounds like a naked romp among Bergman-loving Scandinavian intellectuals only to those with already irredeemably dirty minds.

It is unclear whether the droplet-thoughts of a *thought shower* fall thick and fast enough to warrant the cautious bringing of a *thought umbrella*; nor whether the ideas in a variant phrase *ideas shower* splash more heavily than mere thoughts. *Mind shower*, meanwhile, sounds positively spooky, unless we can think of it as a more rarefied version of a popular disco classic. ('Hallelujah, it's raining minds.')

The more serious problem, though, with *thought-showering* is that it is rarely effective. According to the author and psychologist Keith Sawyer's account of brainstorming, 'in most cases this popular technique is a waste of time'. Unless *thought showers* are carefully planned and directed,

they tend to encourage group conformity and repress
individual creativity. That rather puts the dampeners on
things, doesn't it?

~

touch base

Colleagues and superiors no longer want to 'talk to' or 'phone' or 'contact' you; they want to *touch base*. The first citation of this phrase in the *Oxford English Dictionary* is from a 1918 publication about the American Army in France: 'He had *touched base* at every desk in Headquarters without ever having a chance to discuss the war situation.' The emphasis of *touching base*, then, is on brevity of communication. Just because someone wants to *touch base* with you doesn't mean they are ready to have a half-hour conversation about *Game of Thrones*.

Touching base, of course, is also a term in baseball (it is not clear whether its military use originated as a sports metaphor or the other way around), but to non-Americans the idea of 'bases' is more familiar through American teen movies as a metaphor for feeling someone up. ('Did you get to second base'?) Because of this, so I am told, it makes many office workers in Britain, especially, feel as though they are being constantly pestered by sex creeps. One mischievous *Guardian* commenter suggests the experiment of inserting 'your' in the middle of the phrase. 'Hi,' you can try saying on someone's voicemail, 'I just wanted to *touch your base*.' This would be good for lawyers specializing in sexual-harassment suits, and no one else.

~

town-hall meeting

Everyone loves a villagey cartoon of democracy, which is
presumably why people in workplaces up and down the
land are now groaningly invited to *town-hall meetings*
– which are, er, meetings in which people can raise questions. The phrase seems to have PENETRATED office life
thanks to the *town-hall debates* of American presidential
election campaigns. Of course, these debates are no less
ersatz versions of the 'town hall', since the 'real' people
posing questions to the politicians have been carefully
screened and rehearsed beforehand. Arguably, to get an
authentic flavour of real micro-democracy, *town-hall
meetings* should consist primarily of half an hour of indeci-
pherable ranting from notorious local eccentrics and
busybodies, accompanied by the ambient stench of financial corruption.

~

transitioning

The novelist Cassie Alexander writes of how she once lost a computer-warranty sales job: 'They announced layoffs by taking everyone outside the building and then directing us to certain rooms when we came back in. I got sent into the room where the first slide of the PowerPoint presentation said "*Transitions*" in large italicized font.'

Transitions. What a humane way to announce you are sacking people. By speaking of *transitions* we focus not on the forcible ejection of human beings from our building but on some fuzzy idea of an in-between place – perhaps a moving walkway at an airport – which no doubt leads the *transitioned* person to more exciting adventures.

As with other weaselly and cowardly euphemisms for announcing to someone that they are being fired, saying that people are to be *transitioned* is also quite dehumanizing, since the verb is equally used around the office for entirely non-sentient things. ('We're *transitioning* that product into Calendar 12.') Even so, if you are not being forcibly *transitioned*, you might decide to use the term yourself for a career move ('I've *transitioned* to a new job') just because it sounds so smooth and elegant, as though one were a masterful gliding robot, or a teleporting space adventurer. Me? I shall shortly be *transitioning* to the pub.

~

uplift

Upliftingly, you can now say *uplift* when you just mean 'get'
or 'obtain' – a dismayed man of letters reports that he has
been instructed to 'bring this letter with you to *uplift* your
media access'. *Uplift* as a noun has variously meant an
advertised effect of certain bras, an increase in prices or
wages, and an elevation of the earth's surface; but probably
more relevant here is the idea of moral or spiritual *uplift*.
Perhaps the people in our example are slyly promising that
obtaining your media access will result in an enormous
sense of wellbeing. I rather think that is going to depend
on whether there is an inexhaustible supply of free coffee
and sandwiches.

~

upskill

Have you been *upskilled* lately? It's an odd idea. To say that you will *upskill* a person seems (as with REPURPOSING a worker) to figure the subject as a kind of upgradeable cyborg assistant, into which new programs might at any time be uploaded so as to improve its contribution to profit. We are thus invited to imagine a glorious ascent of a virtual ladder of COMPETENCIES, the better to forget that *upskilling* usually means demanding more work for the same pay. (*Reskilling*, by contrast, means telling someone that what they currently know how to do is redundant, and making them replace it with something else entirely.)

By the way, is there a skill ceiling, a state of being so skill-stuffed that one cannot be *upskilled* any further, or can one *upskill* indefinitely until one is brilliant at literally everything?

~

vertical

Oh, right, the *verticals*. Yep, we need to LEVERAGE the LEARNINGS across all the *verticals*. I'm totally on board with that. Oh, we need to talk about 'content STRATEGY in a difficult *vertical*'? Sure, good idea! [*Sotto voce*] What the hell are *verticals* again?

According to *Forbes*, a *vertical* is 'A specific area of expertise. If you make project-management software for the manufacturing industry (as opposed to the retail industry), you might say, "We serve the manufacturing *vertical*." In so saying, you would make everyone around you flee the conversation.'

In business, there is a distinction between *horizontal* and *vertical* organization. Apple, for example, is sometimes thought of as a *vertical* company because it makes 'the whole widget' – both hardware and software. *Vertical* integration can also be a matter of owning the factories that supply your components, and so forth. Then there is *Forbes*'s distinction between *horizontal* (general) and *vertical* (specialized) markets. In consulting lingo, meanwhile, a *vertical* can just be a new industry that you want to move into, by setting up a separate business unit.

That's a lot of *verticals* to swallow. We might also want to relate all this to the phallic verticality of DRILLING DOWN, if we can bear to. As it happens, in Australian opal-mining, a vertical or near-vertical seam containing the good stuff is called – guess what? – a *vertical*.

The upshot of all this is that *vertical* in ordinary office use can almost always be replaced with 'market', which has the advantage of being a word that everyone understands, and the concomitant disadvantage (for the Machiavellian jargon-wielder) that it won't serve to browbeat and intimidate workers.

Oh, you know what else is *vertical* right now? My middle finger.

~

wagons, circle the

Let's be honest: we're not really travelling in wagons, are
we? We're not Wild West pioneers trying to protect
ourselves from bloodthirsty attacking Injuns by dragging
our caravans into a circular formation and cowering
behind them. The closest I ever get to such a scenario, at
least, is when eating a Wagon Wheel, a delicious round
mallow-and-chocolate biscuit that would instantly crumble
if you ever actually tried to attach one to an axle, so I have
no idea why they are misleadingly advertised as being
suitable vehicular components.

Happily, *Circle the Wagons* is also the title of the four-
teenth studio album by the estimable Norwegian metal
band Darkthrone, which includes such imagistic singalongs
as 'I am the Graves of the 80s' and 'Stylized Corpse'.
Linguistically sensitive office workers should keep a copy of
this record handy so that any suggestion of 'We need to
circle the wagons' can be instantly met by a deafening snatch
of 'Eyes Burst at Dawn'.

~

wash its face

At a literary party (these days, a tragically endangered species of bibulous amusement), a publisher wryly recounts a colleague once saying with satisfaction that some part of the operation '*washes its face*'. Well, sure. A thing has to *wash its face*, right? You can't have grimy-cheeked products or business departments wandering around like pitiable children in a Charles Dickens novel. Or maybe a thing that *washes its face* is supposed to be like an adorable kitten that has learned the basic rules of feline hygiene, licking its paws and then rubbing them repeatedly over its little kitteny fizzog?

Whatever the intended image, to say that something *washes its face* means that at least it doesn't lose you money. It does the bare minimum to earn its keep. Personally, I would require that something not only *wash its face* but also wipe its own arse, but maybe I'm too demanding.

~

weaponizing

According to an article by the partners of Vital Growth
Consulting Group (is that a *vital growth* on your face?
Never mind), it is important to *weaponize* your organization's culture. By 'culture' they don't mean bacteria in a
petri dish, which may be *weaponized* for the purposes of
bioterrorism, but simply the way the people in the
company work together. 'We believe,' the authors write
believingly, 'that as companies become purposeful in
creating a culture, that gives them a competitive weapon.'
They don't go on to explain exactly how this weapon
might be fired; do you load all personnel into a giant
cannon and light the fuse, so that they get fired from the
huge barrel towards the other company, whose own
employees have obligingly formed a human pyramid for
the sole purpose of being knocked over like skittles by the
weaponized flying bodies of their rivals?

It turns out that *weaponizing* things is the ultraviolent
metaphor du jour for office military fantasists. The blog of
an accounting software company assures us that there are
all kinds of '*weaponized* business processes' – including, er,
using good accounting software.

The verb *to weaponize* was first used in a 1957 article in
the *New York Times* by Wernher von Braun – and he should
know, since he invented the Nazi V-2 rocket before going

on to work on ICBMs and space rockets for the Americans. Employees resistant to the relentless glorification of war by management jargon might be interested to know, meanwhile, that the internet contains some interesting advice about *weaponizing office supplies*. Don't mess with me and my Pencil Shooter.

~

workshop

'We're going to have to *workshop* that ISSUE.' Really? Are we
going to dress up in fancy costumes and act out a little
office play? Office types who use *workshop* as a verb probably
imagine doing tough things with hammers and saws and
vices in a sawdust-strewn shed, so picturing the frustrating
immateriality of most modern work as something nostalgi-
cally physical and mechanical. But *to workshop* as a verb is
actually a theatrical usage that dates from the 1970s;
according to the *OED*, it means 'To present a *workshop*
performance of (a dramatic work), esp. in order to explore
aspects of the production before it is staged formally.' So
next time a boss suggests something needs *workshopping*,
gird your loins for the solemn enactment of a brutal
revenge tragedy.

~

X, Theory

In the 1960s, the psychologist Douglas McGregor published
The Human Side of Enterprise, which outlined two approaches
to management. The first approach assumes that people
hate working and crave security, and have to be forced with
threats of punishment to do what you want. The second
approach assumes that people like to make an effort, are
better motivated by rewards, and are naturally creative.

McGregor called these two management approaches *Theory
X* and *Theory Y*. Many unfortunate readers will know all too well
that, despite decades of social science showing that the
authoritarian *Theory X* is counter-productive, it's still quite
common. But why did McGregor choose to call it *Theory X*? Do
people naturally assume that the letter Y (the name of the
cuddly approach to management) is nicer than the letter X?
(Misoandrists who regret the existence of the human Y chromo-
some, which contains instructions to build men, certainly
don't.) To my ears, that *X* makes the nasty *Theory X* sound rather
mysterious and magical, the arena of arcane experts in the fields
of physics or vast alien conspiracies (X-rays, X-Files), and so it
fits perfectly with the general self-glamorizing tone of modern
office jargon. But it is also, of course, a boon to compilers of
lexicons who otherwise wouldn't have anything to put under X,
so you won't hear me complaining any further about it.

~

yield

Don't ever say that your plan will 'give' or 'cause' or 'result in' great things; the only verb to use here is *yield*. Oh yes, there is no doubt that our STRATEGY will *yield* great results. The word probably appeals to management types for two reasons. The first and more obvious is that *yield* is also a noun in finance meaning the expected income from a bond or other holding. The second reason, I suspect, is an obscurely martial or psychosexual one: because *to yield* also means to give way or to admit defeat, the thrusting manager who sees everything *yielding* before him is subconsciously picturing the ground strewn with defeated enemies or willingly passive sex-partners.

~

zero cycles

Zero cycles is how many bicycles you have when you don't
have any bicycles. Perhaps you are a sad clown whose entire
clown act is about lamenting the lack of bicycles in your
clown life. Alternatively you can speak as though you were a
computer that has a finite number of 'cycles' of its internal
clock to perform calculations within a given time. (After all,
since everyone wants to DOWNLOAD to you and enquire
about your BANDWIDTH, you might as well play along.) So
you can say, in response to a request that you do some
extra work: 'Sorry, I have *zero cycles* for this.' It's a splendidly
polite and groovily technical way of saying 'Fuck off and
don't ask me again.'

~

zero-sum game

A *zero-sum game* is any game in which you don't have to do any mental arithmetic, e.g. charades, *Call of Duty*, or Jenga, but not backgammon, darts, or sudoku. (Nor ping-pong or any other sport with points, since I am afraid that even just adding 1 to a score still counts as doing sums.)

Since people now rely on Excel to do whatever sums are necessary, you could call most of modern office life a *zero-sum game*, if it were actually as fun as playing a game. Happily for people who hate maths, it is also possible to make a *zero-sum investment* and conduct *zero-sum negotiations*.

If you insist on being tiresomely pedantic, you can use *zero-sum* in its original sense from game theory, where it means that the outcomes add up to zero. A positive outcome for one player means a negative outcome for the other; one person's gain is another's loss – as in chess or burglary. Oddly, most uses of *zero-sum* in business talk consist of energetic denials that something is *zero-sum*, perhaps because 'zero' sounds rather depressing and unprogressive. 'PCs and tablets are not stuck in a *zero-sum game*,' reports *Businessweek* breathlessly; and the 'Offshore renminbi business', according to the *South China Morning Post*, is 'not a *zero-sum game*' either.

The opposite of *zero-sum* is much more exciting: win-win! Or maybe that's the opposite of lose-lose. Can we just call it a draw-draw and go home?

~

zerotasking

Doing nothing. A consummation devoutly to be wished.

~

SOURCES

The primary sources for dates and senses of words and phrases in this book are the *Oxford English Dictionary* (*OED*) (Third Edition, with draft additions as of June 2013), and Google's Ngram Viewer, which graphs words and phrases over time in all the texts digitized by Google Books. Also useful have been the *Time* Magazine Corpus of American English and the Corpus of Contemporary American English (both created by Mark Davies at Brigham Young University), and other sources where cited in the main text.

FURTHER READING

Carl Cederström and Peter Fleming, *Dead Man Working* (2012)

Melissa Gregg, *Work's Intimacy* (2011)

Victor Klemperer, *Lingua Tertii Imperii* (1947)

Paul Lafargue, *Le Droit à la Paresse* (1880)

Hermann Melville, 'Bartleby the Scrivener' (1853)

Steven Poole, *Unspeak* (2007)

Matthew Stewart, *The Management Myth* (2009)

ACKNOWLEDGEMENTS

The author wishes to thank Paul Laity, Jon Elek, Drummond Moir, Nikki Barrow, Robert Potts, Rosalind Porter, Emma Sheldrick, Anna Richards, Daniel Kellett, Bharat Tandon, Becky Manson, Tony Lezard, Sue Inglish, Julian Loose, Yaniv Wolf, James Miller, Caspar Llewellyn Smith, Pascal Wyse, and Lucien Jones.

The *Guardian* commenters quoted are: Mark Mclauchlan (*alignment*), pilkio1 (*bottom out*), londonscot (*collateral*), lhw123 (*download*), keef1980 (*expectations*), Smoore1 (*helicopter view*), Rotwatcher (*journey*), wumpysmum (*leverage*), Winstone1975 (*robust*), VSLVSL (*sunset*), bhois (*team*), and MJHutchings (*touch base*).